Crafts of Egypt

Crafts of Egypt

Denise Ammoun

Photography
Jean-Louis Bersuder

The American University in Cairo Press

The illustrations from the *Description de l'Egypte* are taken from *Egypt Revealed: Scenes from Napoleon's Description de l'Egypte*, AUC Press 1987.

First published in 1985 as *L'Egypte des mains magiques: artisanat traditionnel et contemporain* by Denise Ammoun

Dar el Kutub No. 2560/90
ISBN 977 424 233 5

Printed in Egypt by The American University in Cairo Press

Contents

Acknowledgments

I should like to thank all those people whose help and advice have contributed to the making of this book, in particular the directors of the Press Center in Cairo; the architect, the late Hassan Fathy; Ibrahim Hussein, director of the Museum of Folkloric Art; Sophie Wissa Wassef; Azza Fahmi, Shahira Mehrez; Marie-Thérèse Ammoun; Huguette Risfoli; Maryse Helal. Special thanks go to Mr. André Azzam, head of the Information Section at the Christian Association of Upper Egypt's Center for Schools and Social Development, whose valuable insights guided me towards a much deeper knowledge of and love for Egypt and her crafts.

For the English edition, I should like to thank, in particular, Stephanie Abboud and Lucy Cooper, who gave it its final touch.

Fatimid Cairo, where past and present exist side by side.

Introduction

Ancient Egypt emerged from prehistory with the arrival of the legendary scorpion king. Land of pharaohs and gods whose civilization enchanted the ancient world, Egypt is a name full of magic and mystery, and a country which demonstrates a continuity spanning centuries.

In the creative acts of numerous artisans, there is, in fact, more than a simple reminder of the past. Through a sort of subconscious memory, their gestures are authentic links between ancient times and the present. This is one of the most intriguing aspects of Egyptian arts and crafts which, in spite of industrial competition, have managed to maintain deep roots in the cities and villages of the Nile Valley.

From the beginning, the River Nile, steeped in history and legend, was the galvanizing element. It was the nucleus of organized life, with its traditions and habits. Already, during this early period, certain handicrafts like basketmaking, pottery, and weaving appeared. According to popular legend, the first weaving apparatus was actually created in Egypt. Isis, one of ancient Egypt's most famous deities, taught her subjects the use of spindle and thread, and some time later, under her divine patronage, they invented the first loom.

In the twentieth century, the descendants of these early Egyptians still excel in artistic trades. They bring us rich tapestries, jewelry of a singular beauty, finely embroidered dresses, and plates of silver or copper worked like delicate lace. From early on, we note the active participation of women, as depicted in pharaonic reliefs. This collaboration continues, with the Egyptian woman often assisting her husband in preparing materials and taking on certain tasks which require great patience or attention to detail. Sometimes she will also participate in the more important and creative aspects of the work. It is the women who embroider their own wedding dresses with talent and poetry, and who create wonderful 'embroidered pictures' in Akhmim, or weave silk in villages across the country. It is also to women that we owe the survival of manual weaving techniques in Nagada in Upper Egypt and in the villages of the Western Desert.

Children are not excluded from this world of arts and crafts. The child-apprentice, to whom the father will divulge the secrets of his craft, is trained with a firm but gentle hand. During the last thirty years in Egypt, the child as creator has also emerged, due, in part, to a fascinating experiment conducted by the architect Ramses Wissa Wassef in Harraniya, a village neighboring the Pyramids (see chapter 3).

Whether individually, in family units or in workshops, tens of thousands of men, women, and children in Egypt, maybe more than in any other country, make their living in handicrafts, almost certainly because crafts here have kept their utilitarian function. And also because this community of artisans has its own particular characteristics. First, there is always recognition of the craftsman-creator, even if most of his fellow workers are indefatigably content to reproduce certain (traditional) patterns, over and over again, with a patience rewarded by an extraordinary dexterity. Second, the Egyptian craftsman is ingenious. He does not demand sophisticated materials to produce his work, is frequently quite happy with rudimentary tools, and has the skill to turn to his advantage objects that in the West would be thrown in the trash. Glassblowers very often use bottle shards to make their molten glass, and in some villages women weave cotton or wool on spinning wheels made from old bicycle parts. The craftsman's characteristic traits are patience, attention to detail, and a serenity in the face of life's difficulties, learned and assimilated, no doubt, through the wisdom of centuries.

If it is not entirely true that industry has dealt a fatal blow to the craftsman, the competition that it has imposed is far from negligible. Certain crafts have continued to flourish, some have slowed down, while others are in danger of disappearing in the coming years. For example, basketmaking and pottery are flourishing, having retained their utilitarian function in the rural areas and poorer quarters of the cities. Weaving and copperwork are also part of daily life and are equally appreciated by tourists and foreign residents of Cairo. On the other hand, art forms such as woodwork, stained glass, and glassblowing are the principal victims of industrialization. So as not to abandon their professions, craftsmen have had to seek employment abroad, in the Gulf States for example, where princes and the wealthy bourgeoisie still appreciate their work. But this 'emigration of artisans' is causing Egypt to lose some of its most skilled craftsmen. Aware of this danger, the Ministry of Culture has created various centers to teach arts and crafts, such as Wekalet al Ghuri and Beit al Sinnari in the center of medieval Cairo.

Cairo's most popular bazaar, Khan al Khalili, is located in the same area. Every day hundreds of tourists flood into this Aladdin's cave, where motley collections of precious jewels, tapestries, silver and copperwork, antiques, and exotic caftans jostle for position. In these narrow alleyways of the *khan*, where cars are forbidden, many languages are spoken, and all sorts of picturesque scenes are enacted, as foreigners make their pilgrimage to this (money-conscious) Tower of Babel. Here, like the ancient pharaohs, they will have their names engraved on gold cartouches, or perhaps they will buy a Bedouin bracelet or an embroidered robe, unaware of the magical charm woven into its design. This bazaar, abundantly and richly stocked with goods, fully reflects the image of Egyptian arts and crafts, the vitality of which is illustrated by the recent rediscovery of the secrets of manufacturing papyrus, which in turn bears witness to the fact that everything can begin again.

1

Clothing

Egypt, cradle of heroes and gods, has seen its share of conquerors, and has endured many wars in its five-thousand-year history. Each significant internal reign has left its mark, and each Mediterranean upheaval has been felt within its territory. But the genius of this country has lain in its ability, civilization after civilization, to accumulate and absorb innumerable social and cultural riches. Today these riches are reflected in many aspects of everyday life, even in the clothes that people wear. Masculine or feminine, national dress even now adheres to precise guidelines, to a tradition of elegance, and sometimes to popular beliefs in which superstition, with all its mysteries, still plays a large part.

The young women of Cairo or Alexandria, squabbling over Bedouin dresses in their desire to follow the dictates of modern fashion, do not realize that the cut of traditional garments, along with their color and embroidery, often have hidden significance. Foreigners blinded by the external exoticism of the clothes share this ignorance. But the adolescent embroidering her wedding dress under the watchful eye of her mother understands the necessity of including a particular motif, a kind of *higab* (talisman against the evil eye) that will protect her against the insidious influence of envy.

4

A craftsman in metal working on a kanaka, *Egyptian coffee pot, wearing the traditional* gallabiya, sideri *and* 'emma.

It is customary for these women to wear black outside the home.

The most well-known traditional Egyptian dress, the *gallabiya*, is worn by peasants, both male (*fellah*) and female (*fellaha*). On the whole, men are not particularly spoiled for choice and each *fellah's* wardrobe is limited to a few items of clothing. Ordinarily the man wears a collarless shirt (*qamis*), large baggy pants (*sirwal*), a vest (*sederi*), and a tight tunic (*quftan*). Over this he wears a long woolen or cotton robe—a *gallabiya*. On his head, the peasant often wears a skullcap (*taqiya*). If he is important, has reached a respectable age, or has a precise function to fulfill, like a sheikh or a mayor, a man wears a skullcap enveloped in a turban (*'emma*).

The cut of these clothes is always identical, only the colors change. A young man will wear a white, pastel, or striped *gallabiya*, while an older man will wear his in more somber tones. Embroidery is rare, found only on the skullcap, the buttonholes of the vest, and the cuffs and collar of the *gallabiya*. This work is done by men and, with the exception of Nubian women who embroider the skullcaps and belts of their fiancés, the tradition is very strict. Male tailors embroider for their male clientèle, and women embroider for themselves. To complete his outfit, the peasant wears leather shoes called *bulgha*, and a wide scarf (*talfiha*) around the neck and shoulders, which gives him a fine air.

The sobriety of men's clothing contrasts sharply with the embroidery, the pleats, the frills, and the jewelry which women display. But in spite of this, the traditional costume of Egyptian men has a style and charm all its own.

As for women, the everyday dress worn by the majority of peasants and working women is a black *gallabiya*. The color is common to many Arab countries and it has a precise meaning. Black signifies respectability, honesty, and dignity. The austere lines of the basic black *gallabiya* of the cities are softened considerably in the countryside, where each dress has a distinctive neckline—round, square, or pointed according to the region—and a yoke from which widening pleats fall to the hemline. The dress, which has no waistline, finishes in a wide flounce, referred to as the *corniche* in colloquial Arabic. Bands of lace, one or several, depending on the financial means of the wearer, separate the bottom of the dress from the flounce. Graceful in its simple form, this model, which is common throughout the Delta, allows for any combination of neckline, lace, color, and pleats of differing widths.

It is important to note, too, that this black dress, found everywhere in Egypt, is just the final, outer layer of clothing. In fact, women usually wear four or five dresses, one over the other, each tailored after the same model. It is a tenacious, rather curious custom, which perhaps originates in Egyptian women's desire to appear robust and healthy. Oriental men are not generally attracted to thin women!

When she is working at home or in the fields, the peasant woman does not put on her black dress, but wears only the charming, flowered garments in which she is most often seen. If she decides to take off one or two of her underdresses, depending on the season or the task in hand, it becomes apparent that her wardrobe consists of gaily colored items. Whether in silk or cotton, velour or wool, each dress is fashioned from colorful, printed fabric.

In principle, adolescent girls and newlyweds wear light colors, even when out of doors or visiting. As soon as her first child is born, however, a woman must respect tradition and dress in black. Once again, in the villages, this custom is more flexible, and in order to preserve her 'best' black dress, the peasant woman will only wear it to go to the weekly market or for a ceremony or official visit. These are twists of etiquette the city woman cannot allow herself, and at the end of the day it is the women like the domestic help in middle-class, suburban homes who uphold tradition. City women cannot challenge tradition even though they walk freely in the streets and work alongside men. Peasant women also meet men in the fields, but in the countryside there is a certain *laisser-aller* missing from city life. No fancy tempers the austerity of the city women's dresses, which have no lace and fewer pleats than those of the villages. Only the jewelry they wear (see chapter 2), identical to that of the peasant women, adds a touch of brightness.

An Egyptian woman's overall appearance is not limited to her dress, but involves numerous accessories dictated by religious morals. If there is no typical hairstyle, it is because women do not generally appear in public bareheaded. To do so might indicate a lack of modesty. Indoors, the woman hides her hair under a colored triangular scarf (*mandil*) bordered by a crocheted edging (*tirtir*) and decorated with a pompom at each of its three corners. Before going out, she hides her *mandil* under a black veil called a *tarha*. After she makes a pilgrimage to Mecca and takes the title of *hagga*, the woman wears a white *tarha*. For more conservative Egyptian women, however, this form of headdress is not enough, and they cover themselves in a long black wrap, something like a sari, often several meters long. This is the *melaya*, though it has different names in different regions. In Akhmim, for example, the *melaya* is known as a *burda*, and in Asyut as a *shugga*. In the past, the face also had to be veiled, so wearing a *burqu'* was obligatory. In the last quarter century this has gradually changed, although the custom still exists in certain villages, in the oases, and in Sinai.

It is a curious fact that until a few years ago, upper-class women in Egypt, unlike other Arab countries, did not like to wear traditional dress except for certain special occasions. Now, however, a new movement is beginning to take hold. It was born under the impulse of a group of cultivated young female artists who were very attached to their national folklore. Despite indignant disapproval from their own social milieu, these pioneers decided to wear traditional peasant dress to various social events. It was, in effect, scandalous and revolutionary, but the interest it aroused in European circles encouraged others to follow their lead. Two of the pioneers, Raya Abu al Eineen and Shahira Mehrez, bought ordinary fabric in the Muski area of Cairo and took it to their village seamstresses, who produced copies of peasant dresses, which the ladies then wore regularly in public. Thus a new fashion was born, which, although rather snobbish, did introduce the traditional dress into cosmopolitan circles.

Bedouin Dresses

While the peasant dress is taking its first steps into upper-class social life, the Bedouin dress is already part of city life. More than a quarter of a century ago, women discovered the charm of these long, black tunics, finely embroidered and often decorated with ancient coins. They come from the oases of Kharga, Dakhla, Siwa, Farafra, and from Nubia, Sinai, and the governorate of Sharqiya, but are collectively called 'Bedouin dresses'. What is not often realized is that these are actually old wedding dresses. Each region of Egypt has its own characteristic wedding dress. Unfortunately, this tradition is being lost, and distinctive models survive only in certain governorates. One notices immediately that, although the decoration varies from place to place, the basic shape, the cut of these dresses, is the same everywhere. (See color illustration 1.) What is more, they also resemble dresses found in Sudan, Libya, Jordan, Palestine and Syria. In effect, they 'speak' a common language of only a few phrases.

This language of clothing has hidden secrets, with certain colors and certain embroidered motifs enjoying magical powers. These popular beliefs are still quite strong in parts of Egypt, being particularly well-rooted in some regions. Often, the fundamental principles guiding the dressmaker are forgotten, but the result has survived. Thus, the adolescent embroidering her wedding dress over months, or even years, knows from her mother that she must embellish it with specific designs. The essential rule is to incorporate a *higab*, in the form of a triangle, into the pattern of the bodice or skirt. Sometimes, the mother-of-pearl buttons, sewn with skill into a dress, play a beneficial role in guarding against the evil eye. The wedding dresses of Siwa are decorated with a multitude of these buttons, which are called 'sun eyes'. Still in Siwa, a white dress is worn the day after the wedding, as white is the color that will assure the young bride a cloudless married life. On the other hand, the color *nili* (like the Nile), a pale green or blue-green, represents a harmful force. There is a superstition that dictates that if a woman in a *nili* dress visits a mother nursing her newborn child, that mother is in danger of becoming sterile unless she hurries to a dyer's and quickly recites a prayer .

For centuries, these popular superstitious beliefs governing women's clothing have been passed down from generation to generation. Today, although they are less deeply held and less widespread, they still survive in villages where wedding clothes have retained a certain mystique.

These dresses are usually long, full, black tunics with no waistline, and decorated with ravishing embroidery. This embroidered decoration varies from region to region. Young peasant girls from villages in the governorate of Sharqiya, for example, have proven to be excellent embroiderers. Their dresses are distinguished by large bands of embroidery composed of triangles and stylized flowers decorating the bodice and a deep hem of the skirt, both front and back. The dresses are skillfully cross-stitched, producing an extremely ornate garment. The sleeves are tight at the shoulder, widening out at the sleeve to resemble the wings of a bird. This cut is exclusive to Sharqiya, and is reminiscent of an image of the goddess Isis who, according to legend, was metamorphosed into a bird in order to fly from one country to another in search of her husband, Osiris, who disappeared in battle.

Sinai, a region of infinite political and religious importance, produces dresses similar in concept to those of Sharqiya. Sinai dressmakers, particularly those from al Arish, also use a cross-stitch in a spectrum of bright colors, producing thick embroidery that trims the bust, hips, and lower part of the dress. This pattern is also very similar to the models worn in Palestine, further proof of an ancestry which unites the countries and crafts of the Orient.

The dresses from Kharga, Dakhla and Farafra, where a very simple stitch is used, are quite different. In general, a kind of feathering effect is achieved using a 'stemstitch' (an overlapping backstitch) and a half cross-stitch to embroider the bodice in vertical bands ending in two horizontal rows of small copper coins. These same vertical rows are found on the sleeves, the sides, and the hem of the dress. The richness of the embroidery depends on the financial means of the woman, so while some dresses are very plain, others are embroidered all over. All of the dresses, however, are charming and elegant.

Moving towards Nubia, dress design shows a noticeable modification. On the bodice of a black silk or transparent tulle dress, naïve, linear motifs representing birds and flowers can be found, perhaps inspired by the pharaonic panels in neighboring temples. (See color illustration 5.) Concerned about their appearance, Nubian women like to exhibit their elegant clothes, and their coquetry often leads to curious scenes. Young Nubian girls, for example, eager to adopt modern fashion from the bigger governorates, wear short skirts with a traditional, embroidered dress of transparent fabric slipped over the top. Tourists who have observed them strolling, parading, through the streets of Nubian towns are unlikely to forget the spectacle!

In Nubia, it is the custom for a woman to embroider her future husband's skullcap (taqiya) and the waistband of his baggy pants (sirwal or sherwal). The skullcaps are finely embroidered, again with flowers and birds, and occasionally a gaily colored hut appears, symbolizing the couple's future home. This picturesque custom has another purpose, as the young bride-to-be often embroiders amorous messages on her fiancé's belt, or wishes him happiness, luck, and prosperity.

Much more luxurious are the dresses of the oasis of Siwa, situated not far from the Libyan border. It was here that Alexander the Great consulted the oracle and was declared the son of the god Amun. The women of Siwa worship elegance and often have the means to indulge their expensive tastes. Not content with only one wedding dress, many women possess seven, a lucky number which also enables them to wear a different dress every day of the week-long wedding celebrations. The dress used in the actual ceremony is basically black, but embellished with embroidery of an extraordinary beauty. The bodice represents the sun from which an infinite number of embroidered lines radiate, studded with the 'sun-eye' mother-of-pearl buttons radiating in different directions just like sunrays. (See color illustration 2.) The dress does not quite reach the ground, allowing the embroidered trousers (*sirwal*) worn underneath to be seen. These *sirwal* are unique to Siwa.

The day after the wedding, the bride wears a white silk dress decorated with tiny suns and sunrays. (See color illustration 3.) In the days that follow, she will wear dresses trimmed with geometric patterns embroidered in chain or cross-stitch. Often the bodice will be decorated with old coins, like the dresses from Kharga and Dakhla. After the honeymoon, the young woman will use this wardrobe for important ceremonies. For everyday wear she has a simple dress of handwoven fabric.

But although one can identify characteristic regional motifs, does the repetition of those very motifs in fact mean that all wedding dresses are a very special, graceful sort of uniform? The specialists, those who can tell the origin of a dress from a glance, would reply in the negative. Certainly a mother gives her daughter advice, guides her work, and sometimes even suggests she copy her own wedding dress. But each girl will imprint her individual personality in the patterns she embroiders. Just as a line of poetry can be interpreted to suit the purpose of each person who quotes it, a dress is never identical to the model which inspired it. Here the embroidery on the bodice will be wider or contain more flowers, there the colors will be less accentuated. Certainly there are general principles, common instructions, a folkloric language passed down from mother to daughter, but there is also a whole gamut of nuances inspired by the emotion of the moment, personal tastes, and individual touches, which make each dress unique. It is this that gives the clothes their distinctive beauty.

Today, foreign women, or even Egyptian women from Cairo or Alexandria, snatch up the dresses made in these regions. It is a mode, a fashion, a fury that will pass perhaps, but this passion has produced an invasion of the villages where humble embroiderers patiently embellish their wedding dresses. Seduced by the offer of money, many middle-aged or older women have agreed to sell their wedding wardrobes. It did not take long for the merchants of Khan al Khalili, Kerdasa, and the large folkloric boutiques of Cairo to take advantage of this interest. As demand increased, these same merchants had the idea of encouraging the embroiderers to take up needle and thread once again. These women, who have long participated in the household economy through their weaving and basketmaking skills, have seized on the opportunity to increase their families' incomes. As a result hundreds of 'falsely authentic' dresses have appeared, pleasing tourists and Egyptians alike.

Kerdasa

In the last few years, Kerdasa, just outside Cairo, has gone even further, becoming the country's main commercial outlet for a range of handmade goods (see chapter 3). Two or three dominant merchants controlling crafts activities in the area began having their embroiderers copy, somewhat crudely, dresses bought in Siwa and Sinai. This 'mass production', which is no exaggeration, has led to the creation of a bastardized style that has taken the name of the village itself. There is now a 'Kerdasa dress', much less expensive than the Bedouin dresses, but popular with tourists on a limited budget.

The quality of this form of traditional clothing is being threatened by such commercial concern. Certainly, wedding dresses that are copied conscientiously in the oasis, or with less care elsewhere, are in danger of losing their freshness and authenticity. The danger is not imminent, however, as long as young women do not concern themselves with supplementing the family budget as they embroider their finery, but continue to dream of the men they will love.

WHERE TO FIND

- Khan al Khalili, Cairo
- Senouhi, 54, Abdel Khaleq Sarwat Street, downtown Cairo
- Gallery Shahira Mehrez, 12 Abi Imama Street, Dokki, Cairo
- Kerdasa
- shopping centers in the large hotels in Cairo
- women's homes in the oases of the New Valley (Kharga, Dakhla, Bahariya, Farafra)
- small stores and the women's homes in the oasis of Siwa
- women's homes in the villages of Sinai, and in small stores in the suqs
- Dresses from all the regions of Egypt are on permanent display (but not for sale) at the Crafts School at Wekalet al Ghuri, in the al Azhar quarter of Cairo.

2

Jewelry

The scene is fascinating. At the entrance to a smelter's workshop, a young boy discards the contents of his burlap sack. Dozens of pieces of silver jewelry cascade noisily from the bag onto the ground. Another boy gathers them up in armfuls and throws them with superb indifference into the dish of a scale. The contents weigh ten kilos. Armed with a heavy hammer the boy then sets about breaking up the pieces, one by one, until the expertly twisted Bedouin bracelets and Arabic-inscribed pendants completely lose their forms. This is the desired goal, as each piece of jewelry should occupy the least possible space in the clay smelting pot (*butqa*), where it will melt and then boil above the burning coals, like any common liquid.

What is most striking in all this activity is the brutality and contempt with which these young apprentices, dressed in dirty ragged clothing, treat the jewelry which must be worth a fortune to them. In the street in front of the foundry, a twelve-year-old boy can be seen carrying a bar of gold on his shoulder as others might carry a bundle of hay. Such spectacles are common in the Sagha, the strongbox of Cairo, where all day long hundreds of artisans prepare the jewelry which all of Egypt will then wear. In this Aladdin's cave, gold and silver are weighed, hammered,

12

pummelled, smelted, and finally returned to their original state as plain metals.

This fascinating quarter does not yield up all of its secrets at once. At first glance the *suq* seems to be a long street of tiny boutiques and jewelry stores, but this is actually the Suq al Sagha, or the goldsmiths' bazaar. From one shopwindow to another, customers are tempted by carefully displayed necklaces and numerous bracelets stacked one on top of the other. The setting is noisy, the narrow street busy with cars, motor scooters, and wooden carts drawn by donkeys and horses. Often the noise of horseshoes on badly laid asphalt prevents financial negotiation, and sales can even fail because of the frustrating, noisy atmosphere. But this is just the façade. The Suq' al Sagha is also, and above all, a succession of small, winding alleyways which criss-cross the entire quarter. It is here that, unknown to the tourists who photograph the jewelry stores for local color, the multiple tasks are performed which lead to the creation of jewelry.

The smelting of old jewelry is effectively the principal resource of the goldsmiths, the means by which they are able to obtain the quantities of gold and silver necessary for their work. This is a direct result of economic restrictions on the importation into Egypt, over the last twenty years, of precious metals, which are subject to precise quotas under strict controls. These measures have almost certainly stimulated a trade, practiced throughout the country, of buying jewelry from the peasants and Bedouins, and turning the items into ingots for reuse. It is thus that the odd spectacle occurs of merchants from the provinces bringing their silver booty to Cairo in a burlap sack. They come to the *suq* area in Cairo, where the largest precious metal foundries are located, and the various procedures begin. After smelting, the featureless ingots are transformed by machine into sheets, plates, and threads of varying width, length, and thickness in the neighboring shops. In the past, smiths undertook this task manually, but today several small factories in the Sagha have the modern equipment necessary to carry out the work for most of the workshops in Cairo.

As if this intriguing preparatory task were not enough in itself, Suq al Sagha is also the area where most Egyptian jewelry is crafted. Alexandria, often called Egypt's second capital, has its own goldsmiths' *suq*, and the models produced there are noticeably similar to those from Cairo and other large cities in the Delta, such as Banha, Mansura, Zagazig, Mahalla al Kubra, Tanta, Ismailia, and Damietta. They each have a jewelers' quarter, but the merchants collect their raw supplies in Cairo. These provincial artisans usually limit themselves to repair work, or to the making of rudimentary jewelry such as rings, plain necklaces, and smooth, rounded bracelets manufactured on an assembly line. By contrast, the jewelers of the oases, of Nubia and of Sinai, have an individuality that deserves special attention.

The Sagha: Headquarters of Egyptian Goldsmiths

To analyze the work that is taking place in the medieval alleys of the Sagha on a national scale, it is necessary to distinguish between the true craftsman, the semiskilled worker, and the assembly-line worker—with the inevitable margin of error involved in such a method of classification.

More often than not it is possible to identify the authentic artisans as those who operate alone or with a limited number of colleagues. Unfortunately this group has very few members, but one never tires of watching these goldsmiths setting a ring with tiny diamonds, or bringing a peacock's tail alive with shimmering, colored stones. Working with a magnifying glass held in the right eye like a monocle, and a pair of delicately balanced pliers, they manipulate all sorts of beautiful gems.

To these craftsmen their work is their passion, as is evident from observing the attention they give to the tiniest detail on a brooch or pendant. Petaled flowers are composed from rubies, crescent moons from topaz, stars from diamonds, and often floral or animal motifs are incorporated into the design, allowing for the maximum use of precious stones. Bracelets, earrings, and necklaces inspired by pharaonic patterns are also created here. If these artisans feel a naïve pride in declaring that they are capable of making any model chosen from a European catalogue, they also occasionally make it a point of honor to create a unique piece.

Repetition, however, is inevitable in jewelry using religious motifs, whether Christian or Muslim, although this does not prevent the artisan from using extraordinary virtuosity as he aligns diamond lettering to form pious phrases in elegant and stylized calligraphy. The phrases most often repeated on medallions, pendants, brooches, and small charms in the form of Koran cases are *Allah* (God), *la ilaha illa Allah* (there is no god but God), and *Allahu akbar* (God is great). This finely inscribed jewelry is the counterpart to variously shaped crosses and medallions representing Christ, the Virgin, or any of the saints who enjoy great popularity in the Middle East. In fact, Islamic or Christian, religious jewelry often dominates the greater part of a jeweler's window display.

Next comes the category of semiskilled craftsmen. Here the tourist is the raison d'être. It is the tourists whose tastes largely determine the artisans' designs and amount of production. Consequently a pharaonic note tends to dominate the market, as most foreigners, whether resident or in transit, dream of taking some piece of pharaonic-style jewelry away from Egypt. Ingenious artisans have been able to exploit this, and the astounding array of jewelry which they offer to their customers is a challenge to common sense. Moving from one shop to another, a recently opened royal tomb seems to stretch before the eyes. Masses of golden cartouches, amulets, bracelets, pendants, and rings are on display. In this context it is the royal cartouche which seems to most inspire covetousness.

The cartouche is an elongated golden loop traditionally containing the last two names of a pharaoh. The artisans are past masters in the art of composing, on an oval of two or three centimeters, the letters of the hieroglyphic alphabet to create the name of Khufu, Ramses II, Seti I, or Alexander the Great. Generally tourists are happy to buy a cartouche inscribed with the name of a famous pharaoh. Recently, however, a new fashion has emerged, as foreigners and wealthy Egyptians increasingly want their own names inscribed on the cartouche. This kind of made-to-order work obviously costs more, but for many people a personalized item of jewelry seems to compensate for the difference in price.

Depending on its dimensions, a cartouche can serve as the setting for a ring, a brooch, a pendant, a bracelet, or earrings. For men they are especially popular as cuff links and key rings. To make these objects the artisan begins work after the machine which stamps the images (be they hieroglyphics, heads of kings and queens, or scarabs) on thin strips of gold. The artisan simply cuts out the letters of the name with a small saw, and watching him gives the impression of a master carpenter at work. His miniature tools are indeed exactly like those of a carpenter. He uses saws, a selection of hammers, and a wide variety of files. In religious silence the artisan manipulates his saw to shape the different symbols (ibis, scarab, arm, eagle or hand) which make up the name of a pharaoh or that of a mere mortal. He then arranges these on the cartouche, solders them skillfully into place, and fits the whole loop into a very fine frame. A final polish and a flourish gives the customer the impression that his piece has its own unique style.

The same technique is employed to make numerous other objects like the scarab (the symbol of resurrection, eternal recommencement), the *ankh* (also known as the 'key of life', to symbolize life and health), the knot of Isis (another symbol of recommencement), and the eye of Horus (symbol of the triumph of good over evil). Using these too, a whole range of jewelry is created in the same way as with the cartouches. Thus the most well-known symbols of pharaonic Egypt are reborn daily in hundreds of copies to the delight of the tourists and with not the slightest touch of creativity necessary on the part of the artisan.

This semiskilled production, pharaonic in character when aimed at tourists, adopts familiar religious or secular themes when catering for native Egyptians. The artisans in this second group copy the models conceived by the goldsmiths, but execute them with much less finesse, and more significantly, with the assistance of machines.

Identical work, insofar as technique and inspiration are concerned, is wrought, in different workshops, in silver. Specialization is clearly defined among the jewelry workers, and there is a clear distinction between goldsmiths and silversmiths. The latter, for obvious economic reasons, are far more numerous.

A separate echelon is reserved for workers in filigree (*shiftishi*) who also have their own workshops. The skill of the artisan in this craft is incontestable even though the threads of silver or gold, which are sometimes as fine as a single hair, are produced mechanically. It is due to the craftsman's precision, patience, and skill, that these marvelous brooches and bracelets with floral, religious, or pharaonic motifs are created. In Egypt most filigree work is produced in silver; gold filigree is very rare. The delicacy of the work is astounding, and only the constant repetition of the same patterns puts *shiftishi* in the category with semiskilled craftsmen.

The reproduction of famous pharaonic jewelry, like the ornamental breastplates, often called pectorals, is generally executed in enamel. These pectorals hang down from a broad chain almost to waist-level, and are designed to depict the falcon with spread wings decorated with lapis lazuli and turquoise, or represent the magic eye surmounted by a solar disc. The originals of these pieces can be admired in their display cases in the Egyptian Museum, but unfortunately reproductions of them are not always so tasteful. The original pharaonic-style necklaces composed of ancient stones found in the royal tombs are much more attractive. Certain jewelers in Cairo are licensed by the government to sell these pieces along with a certificate of authenticity. Modern necklaces that are assembled in Khan al Khalili from precious or semiprecious stones purchased abroad have much less charm.

At the bottom of the 'quality ladder' are workshops of some twenty or so people all performing the same movements almost simultaneously. This is assembly-line work in all its splendor! Here the artisan's job is simply to prepare the mold for rings or bracelets, detach the object from the mold, solder its parts together, and fill the settings for the mass-produced rings with their semiprecious or synthetic stones. Thousands of pieces of jewelry in silver or gold-plated brass, designed for those on very limited incomes, are created here at an unbelievable pace.

Several things may be noted from this tour of the Suq al Sagha. First and foremost, goldwork is evidently still very much a flourishing craft in Egypt. Secondly, it is in this quarter, which resembles an enormous beehive, that the best and the worst are encountered, creativity and repetition, the goldsmith and the simple laborer. Also, just as in the context of clothing, a vast disparity is apparent between the two sexes, so the enormous assortment of jewelry produced is essentially intended for women. In comparison with the abundance of items for women, those for men can be counted on one hand. Across the country, in the rural areas as in the oases, the Egyptian man is content to wear a gold or silver signet ring, perhaps set with a precious or semiprecious stone. In the city he might also be seen wearing cuff links or playing nonchalantly with an attractive key ring. Egyptian men do not seem to mind this inequality, as according to a generalized masculine preference, they are sufficiently proud to have an elegant and richly bejeweled companion by their side.

Popular Jewelry

Artisans who prefer to specialize in popular (in the sense of 'for the people') jewelry can also be found in Suq al Sagha. They have literally hundreds of thousands of customers including the peasant and working classes of the Nile Valley. These artisans make the jewelry worn by peasant women in the provinces of Menufiya, Daqahliya, Gharbiya, and Sharqiya. With only a few exceptions all of the work is done at the Suq al Sagha in Cairo, where merchants from the other large cities regularly go to replenish their stocks. In their turn, these jewelers, who cater for the needs of the neighboring towns and villages, enjoy a large and thriving business.

In Egypt women adore gold, not only because it satisfies their vanity, but also because it represents an excellent investment. Gold acts as a kind of security deposit against divorce, as a woman often takes her jewelry with her if she and her husband separate. This is something like divorce insurance but jewelry is considered more attractive than a bank note! It is, therefore, obligatory that the engagement token (*shabka*) be made of gold. Similarly the gift from a husband to his wife after the birth of a son must also be made of gold. The birth of a girl rarely elicits the same gesture— evidence, if it were needed, of male supremacy in oriental families. Furthermore, when an Egyptian woman buys a gold ring or bracelet, she is effectively banking the money she might have saved over the years. The word *tagmid*, used in such a case, literally means 'freezing' or solidifying', and describes exactly the financial operation the woman is about to undertake.

It is easy to conclude that the style of popular jewelry is sensitive to precise æsthetic concepts, but the first consideration is its weight. The heavier it is the greater the value and the more it is treasured. Having said that, it is easy to understand why Egyptian women dream of possessing one of the heavy semicircular necklaces called *kerdan*, which cover a good part of the upper chest. In its most common form, the *kerdan* includes three or four superimposed crescent moons, embellished with small coins, the whole piece tightly held together with gold links. Other variations present three or more rows of oblong gold pieces, or even minuscule interlaced rings. These models ordinarily have small gold rectangles or lozenges placed at regular intervals to link and consolidate the different rows of the piece. Other less popular models exist, but it would take too long to describe them all. These various necklaces all have one thing in common: they almost entirely cover the chest, but are suspended from a single chain around the neck.

Egyptologists agree that the different types of *kerdan* are derived from the pharaonic pectoral even though gold or gold-plated pieces have now replaced the colored stones of the original jewelry. Sometimes fine filigree work (*shiftishi*) joins or decorates the modern *kerdan*, giving it a Fatimid appearance, as *shiftishi* dates from the Fatimid era.

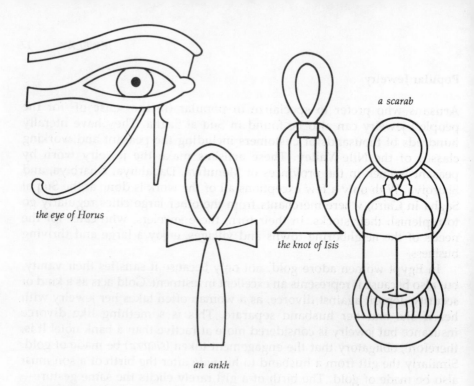

the eye of Horus

a scarab

the knot of Isis

an ankh

A kerdan *embellished with gold coins.*

Because the possession of a *kerdan* is a sign of wealth, an endearing custom has developed in the rural areas. The peasant woman who cannot afford gold instead adorns herself with a gold-plated brass *kerdan*, an exact duplicate of the authentic model, to impress her neighbors. Another necklace favored by peasant women is a single chain of gold beads, sometimes as large as olives (*zeituna*) and at other times as small as chickpeas (*hummusiya*). The women also love to wear necklaces of amber, or if their means are modest, of amber dust, or colored glass. This is a common practice among all Arabic-speaking peoples from North Africa to Yemen.

Wearing earrings is the norm in Egypt, where a girl's ears are pierced almost as soon as she is born. The most popular model worn in this country is that of the crescent moon, called a *makhrata*, the shape of which dates back to the pharaonic era. Sometimes this crescent moon is fashioned in filigree, again combining pharaonic and Islamic influences. Across the Egyptian countryside there is a great variety in the style of earrings (in the shapes of small flowers, hearts, interlaced geometric patterns, and so on) of less precise origin, but undeniably imaginative. This last quality, however, is sadly lacking in the design of rings and bracelets which are, in general, quite plain. The rings are rather crude and heavy in design, as the weight is of primary consideration, and are often set with turquoise, as this shade of blue traditionally has qualities of protection against the evil eye. Bracelets, smooth or textured, are the same as those found in most shopwindows of Cairo.

The peasant woman's collection of jewelry is usually completed by a pair of silver ankle rings (*khulkhal*), sometimes adorned with tiny bells. The weight of the *khulkhal* reflects the financial status of the woman. In the past it was considered elegant to wear two on each ankle to produce a pretty tinkling sound when walking. Previously indispensable, the *khulkhal* is now considered old-fashioned in most regions, and young peasant women are increasingly reluctant to wear this heavy, cumbersome ornament which resembles too closely a pair of handcuffs. Ironically, it is foreigners, tourists for the most part, who are now keen on this kind of jewelry. They wear the *khulkhals* on their arms like enormous bracelets, and the ultimate coup is to exhibit a gold *khulkhal*.

Finally, a special mention must be made of the numerous amulets which women slide into their hair, decorate their jewelry with, and make for their children. The most popular is called *khamsa wi khimesa* (*khamsa* being the Arabic word for the number five). This style of jewelry is probably a derivation of the pharaonic *uzat*, the eye of Horus. It has few variations and is popular among women of all classes.

Specialization is the name of the game among the artisans of popular jewelry, and the workshops tend to choose to make not only a particular type of jewelry, but also a precise style. Some confine themselves to making the *kerdan*, others to some variety of earrings, and yet others to *khulkhals.* The result is, as always, a great dexterity in the work, but how can the repetition of the same movement and the total absence of creative spirit be classed as craftsmanship? These workmen, too, must be grouped among the semiskilled.

Nubian Jewelry

Further up the Nile in the region of southern Egypt and northern Sudan one encounters another race, another ethnic group—the Nubians. Lower Nubia no longer exists. Its ancient temples now stand abandoned on the deserted banks of Lake Nasser, but its villages have regrouped, according to old patterns and following ancient traditions, in areas assigned by the government. Previous neighbors have come together again spontaneously, but there is a perceptible nostalgia that is intensified when the elders recall their memories of the villages which the waters of the Aswan High Dam now completely cover.

Everyday life, with its work and celebrations, has recommenced in Nubia following the traumatic upheaval experienced by its inhabitants. Nubian women, who adore to dress themselves in their finery, again give free rein to their enjoyment of it. All the village women know how to make certain pieces of jewelry and beaded objects. In fact, stringing colored beads is as much a daily pastime for the prosperous woman as it is for those women whose livelihoods, and whose children's livelihoods, depend on this occupation. Girls help their mothers at a very young age, and in every family it is commonplace to see a woman sitting cross-legged making a fan, a small bag, a belt, a purse, a tablemat. The pharaonic influence is quite distinctive in the very wide, colorful bead necklaces they make, which strongly resemble ancient faience pectorals. But other regional influences can also be detected. The pendant-shaped necklace, for example, either in the form of a crescent moon (*makhrata*), or a disc, recalls models from the Delta, the oases, and eastern Sudan. In Nubia these pendants are engraved with motifs depicting birds, flowers, and small houses identical to those decorating their festive dresses. One kind of necklace, composed of a series of small golden discs linked by a very simple chain, is also found in Nubia, but it is rare, as gold is beyond the financial means of the average inhabitant. Nubian women also wear a distinctive, cucumber-shaped amulet as a pendant. It is called a *khiar*, which is the Arabic word for the vegetable it resembles.

Earrings are most often of the *makhrata*, or crescent moon design, but sometimes carefully mounted agates (*sumluk*) of Sudanese origin are worn. It is not so easy to determine the origins of other jewelry found in the region, however, and in some cases even the specialists are undecided. For example, it is impossible to tell whether the rudimentary rings with a central boss, or those with a single stone surrounded by three silver bands, were created in Sudan or in Nubia. Nubian women wear silver bracelets,

In Nubia, every village woman makes bead necklaces.

decorated with small flowers in relief, like those of the Hausa tribe of Nigeria. They also wear the broad bracelets with jutting points that are found in Sudan, but their anklets are almost identical to those of Egyptian peasant women.

A Nubian custom that is gradually disappearing calls on a married woman to decorate her hair with gold or silver coins, small amulets, or even round or triangularly tipped silver chains. Traditionally, a woman also wears a great deal of jewelry on her wedding day, although rising prices now force her to accumulate jewelry over the years. As a result, fewer and fewer weddings are occurring where the dazzling Nubian bride appears covered from head to foot in silver jewelry.

Jewelry of the Oases

Dotted about in the Western Desert like the beads of a huge green rosary thrown down on the sand, the oases of Kharga, Dakhla, Bahariya, Farafra, and Siwa have no more than a hundred thousand inhabitants in total. The population, size, and most importantly, the prosperity of each oasis determines the quality and quantity of the jewelry found there.

The main difference between the jewelry of the oases and that of the villages of the Delta is the absence of gold. The modest life led by the inhabitants of the oases does not permit careless spending. Women cannot afford gold jewelry and must often use base metals instead of even silver. But this relative poverty prevents neither fantasy nor coquetry, and the jewelry of the oases has its distinctive styles. Numerous necklaces are found composed of a silver or metal disc decorated with primitive engravings. The most popular patterns are blades of wheat, palm leaves, flowers, fish, birds, or phrases to guard against the evil eye. Colorful glass beads also inspire unique designs. The bracelets, very wide and carrying motifs identical to the necklaces, are called *domlug*. Ordinarily a woman wears a *domlug* on each wrist. Earrings and rings are often pear-shaped, and decorated with motifs similar to those on the necklaces.

This jewelry is made by skilled artisans of the different villages using rudimentary tools and their own innate talents. They also make long chains ending in small coins which many women slip on under their veils in such a way as to show off the small coins scattered nonchalantly over their shoulders. One custom, now on the decline, is the wearing of a gold nose ring (*gatar*). (See color illustration 6.) This is the only exception to the general use of silver or base metals. Gold is indispensable for these rings because inserting silver through the flesh in a region of the face rich in blood vessels may invite serious infection. In general, however, women no longer show much interest in wearing the *gatar*.

Siwa, the richest and most famous oasis, has a distinctive style of jewelry. Situated near the Libyan border, the region is well-known for its beautiful landscape and its elegant women. It is a prosperous area for various reasons, the most important being the trade with Libya practiced by its inhabitants. The Siwans' buying power is reflected by their luxurious clothing (see chapter 1) and jewelry. A Siwan bride often wears jewelry weighing between three and five kilos depending on her wealth and social rank. Describing this jewelry, the heart of her capital, is in itself a task! On her chest the young woman wears an enormous silver disc (*idrim*) which reproduces the familiar patterns of the oasis. On her wrists she wears a pair of *domlug*, while each of her fingers is graced by an unusual round, square, or triangular ring. The heaviest of these, naturally called 'the wedding ring', has a setting measuring some five centimeters in diameter. The Siwan woman's hair is adorned with various ornaments including tiny cucumber-shaped *khiar* amulets and silver chains with small coins at their ends. Heavy earrings, round and wide, complete the picture. After her marriage, the young wife will buy other jewelry for herself, including rings, pendants, or bracelets like those of the Kharga and Dakhla oases. This jewelry will be almost exclusively silver, because the wealth of the villagers usually precludes any need to buy base metals.

One danger, however, does threaten Siwa. In the last two decades, the development of transportation has brought this distant oasis closer to the rest of the country. The merchants from Khan al Khalili, on exploratory trips, have suggested to the women that they replace their unusual silver jewelry with gold pieces in peasant designs. And the charm of gold has proven to be effective! A number of the women have exchanged their *idrim* and *domlug* for the simpler *kerdan*. This barter enabled the merchants of Khan al Khalili to sell authentic Siwan jewelry, which in turn attracted to Siwa those merchants who specialize in the sale of authentic Egyptian pieces. They buy Bedouin jewelry, but they have also encouraged local craftsmen to step up their production. It is a laudable initiative, which has helped to reestablish a traditional craft in this ancient town, once one of Cleopatra's favorite places.

Alongside this sort of renaissance, a small number of artists in Cairo began to revive the past, as a fine art. These artist–artisans designed and crafted reproductions of pharaonic and Islamic pieces of jewelry. In this context, it is essential to mention the admirable work of Andrée Fahmi, who pioneered this development. Other artists (listed below) have followed suit, giving a new breath of creativity to jewelry inspired by Islamic and Bedouin tradition. (See color illustration 7.) And there are more, those who are guided by the natural shapes of semiprecious stones to compose beautiful pieces of modern jewelry. There is a real resurgence of this sort of work these days—proof, if it was needed, of the marvelous continuity which is characteristic of Egyptian craftsmanship.

WHERE TO FIND

Jewelry made in Cairo
- the Sagha, and neighboring streets, Cairo
- Khan al Khalili, Cairo
- Kerdasa
- the Sagha in Alexandria
- *suqs* of Luxor and Aswan

Jewelry made in the Oases and in Sinai
- Khan al Khalili, Cairo
- Senouhi, 54, Abdel Khaleq Sarwat Street, downtown Cairo
- Gallery Shahira Mehrez, 12, Abi Imama Street, Dokki, Cairo
- Safarkhan, 6, Brazil Street, Zamalek, Cairo
- Nomad, shopping center at the Marriott Hotel, Zamalek, Cairo
- Kerdasa
- stores and craftsmen's homes in Siwa
- craftsmen's homes in the oases of the New Valley (Kharga, Dakhla, Bahariya, Farafra)
- *suqs* of the tourist centers of Sinai (Sharm al Sheikh, Nuweiba, al Arish)

Nubian Jewelry
- Nubian *suq* of Aswan
- homes of villagers in Nubia

Modern Jewelry of the Artist–Artisans of Cairo
- Azza Fahmi, Al Ain Gallery, 13, al Hussein Street, Dokki, Cairo
- Alaeddine Zaki, 16 Sirghani Street, Abbasiya, Cairo
- Suzanne al Masri, 49 Farid Simaika Street, Midan al Higaz, Heliopolis, Cairo
- Ihsane Nada, 35 Wizaret al Ziraa, Dokki, Cairo
- Nimette Riad, 1, Behler Passage, downtown Cairo

3

Weaving

Egyptians like to claim that the art of weaving was born on the banks of the Nile, and that, according to legend, it is to the goddess Isis that we owe the invention of spinning. Isis, one of the most famous of the local pantheon, is said to have taught her subjects the use of the spindle and distaff, and they, under her protection, then created the first loom.

The story is not lacking in charm, but legend aside, Egypt was certainly one of the first and best weaving centers in the ancient world. Some of the oldest known fragments of linen were found in granaries in the Fayoum, and what is more, this was in a country already famous in antiquity for the fine quality of its cloth.

Weavers for thousands of years, the Egyptians first invented a very primitive horizontal loom made of two fixed bars placed on the ground, with the warp threads stretched in between. The weft was inserted by hand until the idea of the heddle (the moveable frame which holds and separates the warp threads) and the comb were conceived. Progress came in successive steps. Craftsmen, who initially did not know how to dye linen (they rarely used wool as it was considered an impure material), learned how to use organic colorings, and subsequently made beautiful cloth. Quite

25

soon, cities like Akhmim, Babylon (Old Cairo), Fayoum, and Antinoopolis established a worldwide reputation for weaving.

While Christianity was spreading in Egypt, the Coptic weavers of the Nile Valley, already masters in the arts of mixing colors and working in linen and wool, invented new methods. Contrary to their ancestors of the pharaonic era, who were unable to weave complicated patterns, the Coptic weavers broke triumphantly away from the old styles, and produced an array of patterns that left their imprint on the history of Egyptian weaving. Using advanced techniques, they succeeded in weaving cloth with designs inspired by ancient Egypt, Hellenistic Greece and occasionally by Persia. Specifically Christian motifs, like crosses, fish, lambs, sacred vessels or portraits of the saints, were quite rare. All these designs, made possible by the new sophisticated techniques, were the origin of the famous 'Coptic textiles' which museums are so proud to possess today.

From the beginning, the Islamic world greatly appreciated Egyptian textile manufacture. The Abbasid caliphs, quick to recognize the potential, dominated the Delta centers of Tanis, Alexandria and Damietta. Workshops, official or private, were in the pay of the caliphs of Baghdad and under the control of their agents. In 870, the coup d'état of Ahmed Ibn Tulun put a stop to this exploitation. Egyptian weavers were henceforth to work for their own country. The Copts continued to work and develop their style, while their Tulunid colleagues wove bold human and animal figures. Correctly speaking, the true Islamic period begins at this point. It represented 'a new broom', a fresh way of looking at the world. Of course, as with all art forms, during the early centuries, the Muslim artisans drew inspiration from the examples that came before them, especially from Coptic art. Later, the Islamic craftsmen would assimilate these borrowings to create their own style. By manipulating ancient formulae in new combinations and adding their own personal touches, they created one of the gems of Islamic art, that very special art form where the Islamic soul is expressed through rich colors and images.

Weaving experienced brilliant growth under the Fatimid sultans. It was in the middle of their era that the weavers began to abandon the drawings of men and animals so prevalent in Coptic patterns, and switched to geometric, floral, and inscriptive decorations. This foreseeable evolution was the only radical change. Apart from that, weaving continued to be, as it had been since the time of the pharaohs, a domestic craft, in which each member of the family performed a precise function.

Unfortunately however, little by little, Egyptian fabrics ceased to cross the seas to enchant the ancient European civilizations. There was a decline in the quality of the work, which can perhaps be attributed to Ottoman domination. The sultans called the best artisans from their empire to Constantinople. This, without a doubt, harmed local production. Another serious reason for the decline was that many important artisans

left *Did the goddess Isis teach Egyptians how to spin?*

bottom left *Sorting threads, with a facility born of the continuity of ages.*

bottom right *Spinning at home is a common sight here in Gurna, as in all the centers of weaving in Egypt.*

A weaver's studio from the late eighteenth century, showing looms which had changed little since pharaonic times, and have not changed since the picture was drawn. From Description de l'Egypte.

made their way to Europe. Thus, even before the massive competition from mechanical weaving, Egyptian fabrics no longer enjoyed the same prestige abroad.

But the weavers who did not leave Egypt did not abandon their profession. They continued to ply their looms with the same fervor, no doubt because the love of weaving, and the patience that it requires, flows in the veins of Egyptians. This perseverance enabled weaving to make a dramatic comeback in the twentieth century, both as a craft and as an industry.

In the industrial sector, weaving is incontestably one of Egypt's strengths, as cloth constitutes 66 percent of Egypt's export trade. There is no question that Egyptian cotton enjoys international fame. And parallel to industrial growth is the revolution in weaving as a craft. The local initiative inspired by Ramses Wissa Wassef has enabled the weavers of Harraniya, Kerdasa and Garagos to claim world interest once again.

Akhmim

At this point, the question is raised of which cities and centers have survived this long passage down the centuries. Babylon has not survived, nor has Tanis. Antinoopolis, founded by the emperor Hadrian in memory of his favorite, Antinous, is now just a village called Sheikh 'Ibada opposite the small market town of Roda, south of Minya. The Fayoum has experienced more than its share of alarm and change. Among all the weaving cities of antiquity, the only one remaining today is Akhmim, known to the Greeks as Panopolis. What is more, it has retained its position as the largest weaving center in Egypt, with five hundred weaving looms and the largest concentration of weavers.

To stroll about the streets of Akhmim is to go back in time. The ancient streets are the living images of the past. In most houses, some still without electricity, weaving is still a family activity. Father, mother and children congregate around the loom. Sometimes, through an open door, the weaver can be seen doing his work at an archaic loom, worthy of a place in a museum of folklore. He throws the shuttle back and forth while listening to a song of Omm Kalthum, the nation's most famous singer who, even though she has been dead for over two decades, has not stopped vibrating in the hearts of the Arab masses. The artisan's little boy, called the *gabbad*, assists him by carefully keeping the warp threads straight and taut. In a corner of the room, his wife spins cotton with a rudimentary spinning wheel or a distaff, or perhaps she is filling the bobbins with thread taken from the spinning wheel. At other times the weaver and his wife can be seen seated on the ground, opposite each other, setting up the loom by slowly passing warp threads through the heddle. Their collaboration gives the impression of silent complicity. Artisan couples acted no differently in the days of the pharaohs. In fact, working methods have not changed for thousands of years. But unfortunately, times have changed. With the coming of the twentieth century, machines have replaced men, often driving them away from their looms because they were without the courage or the means to surmount the problems of maintaining the same lifestyle, while keeping up with new production flow. In spite of this, the weavers of Akhmim are loyal to tradition. They continue to weave linen, wool, cotton and silk.

If we look more closely at the results of the weaving of the craftsmen of Akhmim, we will be able to analyze a particular type of cloth, as well as to give a clear description of the methods employed. With the exception of very few differences, methods are identical for all types of weaving in Egypt. The working methods are the same and so is the full family collaboration.

As for traditional patterns, they are found everywhere, with varying degrees of alteration from the original. Whether in fabrics, carpets, or tapestries, geometric and floral patterns dominate the greater part of the weavers' work. Epigraphy is not widespread. And the representational style which enables popular tapestries to describe the environment is not foreign to the themes of past centuries.

But, to return to Akhmim and to the operations which precede the weaving itself. The many preparations of the raw material are made by the women; cleaning the cotton or the wool, spinning, winding the bobbins, and preparing warp threads of equal length have been women's tasks since

With just a few exceptions, weaving methods are the same all over Egypt.

earliest times. But at the final stage, the setting up of the loom, it is the weaver himself who directs operations. It is he, too, who chooses the colors, with a marked preference for ochre and purple which he combines to perfection. The patterns, which are repeated along the length of the cloth, are two to three centuries old. They are known by many names: scorpion, stars, the great scorpion, diamonds, diamonds with a central cross, 'biscuits' (an interlacing diamond pattern), 'sikhs' (a design of superimposed scorpions), and more. If they do not reproduce exactly the designs of the Coptic fabrics of the third and fourth centuries, it is evident that they have evolved from them.

In the past, the weavers of Akhmim restricted their work to making broad wraps (melayas) or fringed cotton shawls striped in bright colors, which were, and still are, worn all over Egypt. But with the technical and social assistance of the Upper Egypt Association, which has been active in the region for about twenty years, the artisans have learned to make reversible bedspreads (highly prized by both local and foreign clientèles), tablecloths, and napkins. They have also learned to take advantage of a larger assortment of colors. All of this has contributed to improving their production and expanding the local market to an international one, which in turn, has considerably raised their standard of living.

Unfortunately, this type of individual assistance will not guarantee the future of the weavers. To reach this goal, aid, preferably from the government, seems necessary. All the more so because, although weaving survives in many regions, the conditions of its survival are difficult. Handweavers will have to withstand competition from mechanical weaving by selling at a higher price, because they can offer the dual advantage of better quality and different products. At the same time, artisans must try to outmaneuver the exploitation of workshop owners and wholesale merchants, and assure themselves of a regular clientèle. In short, they have a fight on their hands.

Looking at the expansion of this craft in Egypt, it can be seen that the weavers have decided to wage their combat with great courage. In fact, they are becoming active just about everywhere, in the cities as well as the villages. The result is that weaving continues all over Egypt, even if on a very reduced scale and strictly for local needs. It would be absurd to try to mark a map of Egypt with centers of 'types of weaving'. It would be overcrowded and inaccurate. Inevitably there would always be forgotten villages and unknown quarters, where a solitary weaver has not abandoned his own regional style of production. In the context of weaving, as in that of pottery (see chapter 8), this type of map is a trap to be avoided. It is much more practical to restrict oneself to a few landmarks, indicating more generally the regions known for their work (even when they are inaccessible to the ordinary visitor), and marking only concentrations of particular types of weaving, such as Harraniya, Kerdasa, Garagos—to name just a few.

Other Weaving Centers

If the trip is to begin in Upper Egypt, Nagada may serve as a parallel to Akhmim, and constitutes a very striking example. A small village, with no real roads or modern means of transport, until recently Nagada was visited only by archaeology buffs attracted by the discoveries made in a neighboring necropolis. Now though, Nagada boasts a second attraction, as, thanks to its women, weaving survives in the brown stone houses of this village. Without a doubt, it is a unique case in Egypt. For a very long time the weavers of the village made silk and wool cloth, primarily for the cities of Sudan. But the establishment of a mechanical weaving factory at Qus (the district's main town), on the opposite bank of the Nile, signaled the end for all the handweavers of the region. The risk of seeing their looms empty and unproductive was great. It was then that the women reacted with audacity. They did not hesitate to put their hands to the small, rather rudimentary, fixed-warp weaving looms. Using these, they produced, with as much skill as the men, the type of silk *melayas*, with a black background crossed by threads of silver, gold, or wine-red, with which Sudanese women are so smitten. (See color illustration 12.)

The weavers of Garagos, those who do not come under the tutelage of the center created by Father Ackermann (see below), also work with the Sudanese women in mind. These weavers, working for themselves, weave smaller (three meters x 90 centimeters) pieces of artificial silk called *firka* in parallel red, yellow or black bands. A little farther away, at Sohag, many weavers have resisted the temptation of getting a regular salary by becoming ordinary workers in a mechanical weaving factory established in the city. They preferred to take up the challenge to continue the production of cotton cloth similar to that of Akhmim.

Another center which has remained important over the centuries is located at Asyut. In this city, the largest of Upper Egypt, the weavers primarily make a medium-quality floor rug decorated in floral or geometric patterns. Their carpets are of a good quality of workmanship, though of no creative worth, as templates of Persian designs are strictly followed. Rugs and carpets produced in Asyut are used all over Egypt, but are not exported. In particular they are found in the stores of Cairo, Alexandria, and Mansura. It is the same at Kutna and Kom Gharib, and in numerous other villages of Upper Egypt. In contrast, at Geheina, weavers and villagers, through a strange complicity, have adopted the same patterns for the walls of the houses as they have for their carpets. Rectangles or bricks of ochre, red, yellow, and brown create harmonious patterns on both walls and carpets. Unexpectedly, the weavers have inspired the masons, a reversal of the usual order of things, and not lacking a sense of fantasy and interest.

This is more or less the style found at Beni Suef and in the Fayoum. The weavers of these two regions create marvelous little rugs using a tasteful blend of geometric designs in red, green, white and black. Prayer rugs (*mihrab*), so widely used in Egypt, are also woven in the Fayoum. Those made elsewhere, in some quarters of Cairo, Fuwa, and in the villages of the governorate of Menufiya, employ the colors of the raw wool—white, beige, dark brown, and black—and do not possess the spark or vivacity of those made in the Fayoum. This may be the essential distinction between the many varieties of rugs.

It is the women, again, who deserve praise, when one leaves the Delta to visit the oases. In Siwa, as in Kharga and Dakhla, it is the women who weave goat's wool into small, brightly colored Bedouin rugs. The patterns are made up of bands and stripes juxtaposed in such a way as to constitute a recognizable motif. Finally, in the villages of the Western Desert, such as Borg al Arab and in the area around Mersa Matruh, the women produce some very beautiful woven rugs in remarkably restrained designs of lines and diamonds on a background of red, white or navy blue. In certain villages of the Eastern Desert, the same work can be found, characterized by an absence of symmetry coupled with imaginative arrangements of geometric motifs.

In spite of the difficulties it faces, weaving is still a flourishing activity in Egypt. This is why the twentieth century is witnessing a series of exciting, innovative approaches. They are transforming the art of tapestry and restoring the Coptic tradition of weaving through rugs made by children.

Harraniya and Ramses Wissa Wassef

Harraniya is a village which owes its fame to one man, the architect Ramses Wissa Wassef. Today people come from Paris and New York to visit the famous white-domed atelier which houses weavers of all ages. A basic curiosity as well as a love of art entices people here to watch the work of these artisans, who are known for both the originality and the beauty of their craft. Visitors go, as if on pilgrimage, to the rooms where the weavers, often very young, sing to themselves as they play with shapes and colors to recreate the world as they know it.

The success of Harraniya is the result of a long struggle by Wissa Wassef. These children, who weave such marvelous tapestries, who project the world of their imaginations into images at the loom, are the proof that we are all born with an artistic ability, and—if the definition of craftsman is "one who produces useful and beautiful objects"—that crafts can hold a place in the twentieth century. These are the ideas the architect has defended over the years and which constitute his doctrine, more or less. The result of intense research, this so-called 'doctrine' is the touchstone of the thrilling experiment at Harraniya. Because of the undeniable influence which Harraniya exerts, not only in Egypt but internationally, this enterprise and the circumstances surrounding its birth and development deserve a deeper look.

In the beginning, during the forties, Ramses Wissa Wassef, still a young architect, rejected the attitude which gave mediocre status to the artisans in modern society, and which viewed their activities with scorn. He rebelled against many prejudices and definitions. How can it be claimed that, "the artisan is simply a manual laborer," when many artists choose to exert considerable manual labor to create their works? Similarly, how can it be stated that, "the artisan merely produces copies"? There are as many artisans who are true creators as there are artists who are mere technicians. Does the difference lie in the fact that the artist is able to force his notoriety on society? Not at all. No definition convinced him and he continued his stand against the notions of major and minor art.

Bringing all of this into question induced Wissa Wassef to haunt Old Cairo, the ancient seat of crafts in Egypt, to look closely at the activities to be found in the workshops there. It was there that he hoped to find the answers to his own questions. He met artisans of whom no one took notice any more, people who were thrilled to discuss their work with someone who showed real interest. He quickly noticed that potters, glassmakers, and weavers were stuck fast in obsolete ruts, that the 'language of styles' they used no longer responded to modern tastes, and that they were incapable of updating or of creating. Several of them had not even trained replacements to follow them, since their profession was no longer viable in their eyes. Under these conditions, how could they revive their crafts? On top of this, the financial measures taken by the government appeared equally sterile to him. Subsidizing the artisans would not solve their problem. Some of them had a craft which had responded to society in earlier times, but the progress of society, notably under the influence of industrialization, had transformed the context in which they worked. Not geared to adapting to the new parameters by modernizing his methods, the traditional craftsman was doomed to extinction. By dint of investigation and analysis, Wissa Wassef evolved a scheme which he believed would improve the situation. "Craftsmanship is the work of an individual on chosen materials in order to produce a beautiful and useful object," he wrote.

Wissa Wassef's activities were guided thereafter by this formula, as by several similar principles. In the first place, he insisted on attempting his experiment with the young and receptive, those still untouched by the school system. He criticized state and private teaching for the use of authoritarian methods, which often threatened to paralyze the judgment and sensitivity of children. It was towards them that he directed his efforts, because he had a profound conviction that, "everyone is born an artist. But, in order for him to take advantage of his gifts, artistic creation must be an integral part of a craftsman's life from childhood on." He was equally sure that art and craftsmanship can coexist perfectly in the same activity, and that any crafted object can find a serious clientèle as long as it is useful and interesting. Finally, the essential principle which kept him going was the certainty that any child could find his or her own style of artistic creativity if placed in an environment which allowed his or her gifts and creative drive free expression.

At that point, he set himself to determining the type of craft which would offer the children a relatively simple technique. In the end he chose weaving, and in particular, tapestries. He had specific reasons for his choice. "I saw in it the means of allowing a child to produce an image using a technique belonging to the field of crafts; that is to say, an activity based on a union of the soul and body, a balanced fusion of art and manual work . . . . To children, images are the vehicle of their emotions, the reflection of their psychic lives. It is just as easy for them, just as natural, to express themselves through images as through language, which to them is no more than a succession of images."

There was nothing left to do but apply his theories. Circumstances helped him. The Committee of the Association of Coptic Schools decided to found a learning establishment in Old Cairo. Engaged to draw up its plans, Wissa Wassef called in masons from Aswan, skilled in constructing domed houses in brick, according to procedures in use since the first pharaonic dynasties. And so a building resembling those of yesteryear raised its domes into the sky above Fustat. Then Ramses Wissa Wassef and his father-in-law, the renowned artist Habib Gurgi, proposed the philanthropic venture of training children in artistic techniques. In this the architect saw the opportunity to put into practice his theory of the fusion of arts and crafts. From the time when he had made his fundamental choice, he had learned to weave. He preferred, however, to leave the instruction of his students to a professional weaver. The old man, one of those whom he had met during his wanderings in Old Cairo, was perfect for the job. Very soon a few pupils with talent emerged from the main group. In guiding their steps and following their development, Ramses Wissa Wassef began to realize that he would dedicate his life to this experiment.

And the Coptic School was just the beginning. Now Wissa Wassef wanted to launch his experiment on a much grander scale. With his wife Sophie, a trained painter, joining wholeheartedly into his adventure, he wanted to work with the young *fellahin*. The sacrifices that had to be made and the risks that could result in failure did not dull their enthusiasm. They decided to open a studio in the middle of a village. Harraniya, a minuscule peasant village, close enough to the capital, appeared to be an ideal place. Although located only fifteen kilometers from Cairo, this village had escaped the corruption of modern influences. The children who inhabited it had therefore not been exposed to the fever of the city; their freshness and vision had been preserved—indispensable ingredients.

Ramses Wissa Wassef bought a plot of land of approximately three thousand square meters in Harraniya, right next to a canal where the ducks and geese splashed about happily and noisily. While the walls of his studio went up, thanks to the masons of Aswan who had built the school in Old Cairo, the architect and his wife began to make contact with the village children. Like all children in all the small villages of Egypt, those of Harraniya were thrilled to meet strangers, a sure source of entertainment. In fact, in this couple, they found play companions and, above all, inexhaustible story-tellers. About fifteen of these *fellahin*, those who came regularly, learned the most beautiful stories belonging to local folklore, and became attached to their new friends. As soon as the studio with the white domes was finished and had taken its place in its setting in the countryside—like a jewel in its case—the architect explained his plans. He asked *all* of the children, with no attempt at or thought of selection, because he was sure that creativity was equally present in all of them, if they would agree to work with him. The response was enthusiastically positive. Nothing remained but to engage Myriam Hermina, an excellent student from the time of the Coptic school, to come once a week to teach them weaving. Just as with the old weaver, she was asked to limit her teaching to basic techniques.

A few months later, when the young apprentices had assimilated all the procedures of weaving, the role of Ramses Wissa Wassef began. He was dealing with children who had not been subjected to the corruption of received ideas, and who were still able to look at the world through the eyes of innocence. It was a rare privilege. He allowed himself to give them only one bit of advice, suggesting that they recreate on the tapestries, the trees, birds and houses which were the framework of their existence. Then he encouraged them to do as they wished, to choose the colors which attracted them, to bring together seemingly incongruous objects, like a donkey and a fish! The power of the imagination exceeds all logic and attains marvelous poetry. How can one dare to paralyze invention in the name of realism! Further, his experience at the Coptic school enabled him to formulate three fundamental rules. The first was not to give the young weavers a pattern to follow, because, in his opinion, making a sketch or preparing a model for a work of art split the creative act in two, and gave an opportunity to sidestep a difficulty. He was categoric on this point. "Only the risk implicit in creating the real thing can allow creative effort to evolve and succeed." He defended his other two principles with the same vigor. He insisted on withdrawing all exterior æsthetic influences from the environment of the children, in order to avoid the slightest temptation of plagiarism. He also barred the intrusion of criticism or adult interference, in order to protect the children from doubts which could engender value judgments of their work.

It is obvious that one does not have to agree with this ideology, yet it worked in the case of Harraniya, where Wissa Wassef applied it with an unshakable faith. For days on end, he watched the children struggling at their looms; he was a silent spectator to their stumblings, but he never refused to help when asked for advice. And then he saw a young weaver create his first pattern. Monstrous bird or deformed animal, that was of no importance! An image was taking form directly on the loom; it was pure creation. The joy expressed by the children at their first attempts was indescribable! That of the architect and his wife was no less. They had won their artistic bet. Now everything was possible.

Through perseverance the quality of the work improved. Just as children progressively enrich their vocabulary, young artists refine, polish and perfect their techniques of drawing and composition to develop their individual styles. From the moment when the work was the least bit interesting, Wissa Wassef rewarded the creator. In his eyes, this procedure offered multiple advantages. It allowed the children to gain self-confidence and to value their skill, as that was what had earned them their money, and at the same time it proved to their parents that they were engaged in a profitable job. He also saw it as a way of grading work, of rewarding and stimulating the creative effort. To administer this dual-purpose reward scheme fairly, he perfected a system: the price which he paid was calculated on the length of the weaving, multiplied by the care taken with the work, and the beauty of the piece. A judicious means of recognizing the relative values of originality, care and attention, and perseverance. On the other hand, this method discouraged mediocre production. As an added advantage, it freed the architect from supervising the work—a job he found repugnant—and instilled a sense of liberty and responsibility in the children. They worked as they wished, chatting and singing if they so desired, or taking more breaks to go and play in the garden. Only the final results counted, and this they knew very well.

In the afternoons, the weavers returned to their homes and again became little *fellahin* like the rest. Occasionally they helped their parents in the fields or at home, and were absent from the atelier for a day or two. But through all these ups and downs, each tapestry was slowly born. Trees, people, fairy-tale animals all took the places assigned to them in the imaginations of the weavers. From time to time the children experienced the same sorts of tribulations as adult artists do. They passed through phases of depression, and of stagnation. Sometimes they tended to repeat themselves or to copy their comrades. This was a warning signal. They had to be relieved of this stupor, and have their imaginations restimulated in some way. On these occasions Ramses and Sophie Wissa Wassef immediately planned a trip into the country, to the zoo, into the city, or organized a picnic on the banks of the Nile. Then life went back to normal again in Harraniya, in a joyful atmosphere which could be read on the faces, and was reflected in the work.

Six years slipped by happily in this way, and the talent grew. By 1958, the weavings of Harraniya demonstrated a consummate technical skill combined with a naïve freshness and vigorous inventiveness, which created a fund of inexhaustible poetry. (See color illustration 8.) Some works contrasted with others, moving away from fantasy to launch into a rigorous reconstruction of reality, others began to exaggerate the characters of the people or animals—to make the sorcerer more monstrous or the tiger more fearsome. Still others concentrated on producing fine compositions. Wissa Wassef judged that the moment had come at last to show the work to the public. The first exhibition was held in Cairo, and aroused lively interest, not among Cairenes, but among foreigners. Then, in the workshop at Harraniya, influential and enthusiastic people organized an exhibition to be held in Basle, and another in Zurich. The interest aroused by the children's work, and the admiration which it provoked, opened wide the doors to the whole world. Year by year, another world capital or important city received the tapestries marked with the initials 'WW', for Wissa Wassef. In turn, Stockholm, Amsterdam, Paris, Geneva, Copenhagen, Milan and London fell under their spell. Dazzling successes were recorded everywhere. This particular style of artistic expression inspired artists and attracted impassioned adherents. It can be said, without exaggeration, that a new artistic school was born.

Coptic Rugs

Coptic tapestries were the glory of ancient Egypt. Ten centuries or so later, Coptic rugs are once again something modern Egypt can boast of with pride. Even if there has not been a total renaissance, these rugs weave a strong bond with the past. They are a reflection of a style which occupies a special place in the history of art, and enriches it with a new element: the weaving of carpets. While the artisans of the early centuries produced fabrics—cloth and tapestries—using linen or wool thread, their descendants renew their ties with tradition, but also adapt to modern circumstances by manufacturing thick-pile woolen carpets in traditional designs.

Strangely enough, the rebirth of this Coptic art form began for reasons a long way removed from art. The Coptic community, whose solidarity is a byword, was disturbed by the plight of large numbers of poor children who were deprived of any form of education, even religious instruction. In 1940, in a philanthropic effort to alleviate this situation, a group of well-to-do ladies formed a committee to found schools in Upper Egypt, a region containing large Coptic communities. The committee acquitted itself admirably in its purpose, and financed a network of free-tuition schools, using money raised through subscriptions and charity bazaars. Later, two schools were even opened in the capital: one in Old Cairo and the other in Mahmasha, on the outskirts of the city. During the fifties, some of the students were taken in hand by Ramses Wissa Wassef.

This architect, who was about to revolutionize the art of weaving in Egypt, began his experiment. He gladly recruited children who showed a penchant for weaving. He put them in his workshop, or turned them over to his father-in-law, Habib Gurgi, who initiated them in the skills of pottery. So, while following a basic education program, these students learned a trade compatible with their aspirations. This fact guided the next initiative of the ladies of the committee of Coptic schools. They had to consider the future of their students. Why not prepare them for a lucrative profession, that of a weaver?

The decision was followed by the purchase of weaving looms. Then the choice for production fell on thick-pile carpets which could easily find buyers. The first motifs woven into these carpets were borrowed from the environment—lotus flowers in various designs. Trained at Wissa Wassef's school, the young weavers quickly produced satisfying results and began to develop a loyal clientèle. It was then that luck intervened. Mrs. Fahim Bakhoum, in charge of the manual work, found a book in her library which was to determine the course of this craft. It was an illustrated work on *The Coptic Tapestries*. Signed by Gerspach and published in 1890, it contained a remarkable study of the subject and included numerous plates of the various designs.

Why had it not been thought of earlier? Since they were dealing with young Copts, endowed with a prestigious heritage, why not teach them to draw on precisely this heritage? The ancient designs could be adapted to thick-pile carpets. In this way, the result would be an original creation which could offer the bonus of reviving the past.

A young draftsman faithfully reproduced and enlarged the designs onto cardboard patterns, but the selection of which designs to adopt was dictated by a sense of respect. The decoration of the original tapestries included figures, flowers and animals. The figures, mostly representing saints, would not be taken up again. And for good reason: the rugs would be walked on, and it would be indecent to tread on a Saint George or a Saint Mark! Apart from this exception, the traditional Coptic patterns were given new life. The floral and animal designs were resurrected with great taste, and the lion—a favorite theme—won favor with the public.

When you go to Old Cairo or to Mahmasha to visit the pupil–weavers, and if you catch them during the hours when they are working in the studio, you may experience the sensation of passing through a time warp! These students are repeating the movements, copying the gestures of their ancestors. There they are, seated in front of a vertical loom manipulating the woolen threads and recreating the models of yesteryear. Further, this craft—at least as it has been conceived in Cairo—does not encourage egotism. The pupils follow each other on the same loom, each one adding his own touch, his personal effort, to that of his colleague, in order to end up with a collective work of excellence. The artisans of antiquity observed similar anonymity. The only noticeable difference shows up in the technique (that employed in making thick-pile rugs is not exactly that of tapestries) and in the choice of colors. Today, the background is light with the design in dark tones, deep brown or black. Previously, the background was purple or brown while the pattern was in blue, indigo, violet blue or sky blue. The style, however, is identical, except for minute alterations in detail or subtle effects, giving each carpet its own character and special attraction.

These Coptic rugs have been in production now for about a quarter of a century, and belong among the notable crafts of Egypt. Sadly they cannot be found on the commercial market because of the limited production—to the order of about ten carpets per year. This state of affairs exists because the members of the committee refuse to consider this craft from a financial standpoint. In their eyes, weaving rugs is but a way of teaching students a profession without pushing them or imposing a production schedule on them. This explains why the rugs are sold as they are produced to friends or to people who anxiously keep watch for the moment to claim them when they come off the loom. However, this does not prevent the annual exhibition in Mrs. Bakhoum's house, which is held even if all the rugs are already reserved. It is a custom which attracts both the curious and the committed.

Garagos

Garagos is a village to which the train does not go regularly. To reach this little island of greenery, which is surrounded by monotonous fields and dominated by Qus, a county seat of Upper Egypt blackened by the smoke of factories, the means of transport can be quite varied. They range from humble carts to the romantic caleche, with bicycles and taxis in between. It is just a matter of covering the six kilometers which separate Qus from Garagos (in Upper Egypt it is pronounced 'Jarajos'), and to follow the 'Montgolfier road', named after the Jesuit father who laid it out in the fifties, and which is occasionally no wider than a footpath.

Instructed by his order to revive the Coptic parish of the village, Father de Montgolfier lost no time in also founding a school. Then he asked himself how to develop careers for those young men who were not rich enough to farm their own land, but who wanted to escape from the plight of simple peasantry. After some trial and error, he opted for the type of craft dictated by local tradition: pottery.

In 1956 Father Philippe Ackermann, whose name would henceforth be attached to the whole Garagos experiment, relieved him. It was he who shaped the way of life through pottery as practiced in the village, and provided the impetus which gave it its current renown (see chapter 8). But, at the same time, he did not forget the young girls. He had noticed that making pottery gave the young boys an opportunity to blossom, giving them a certain autonomy while developing their skills and creative sense. He wanted the girls to share in these advantages. From both a humanitarian and a social standpoint, it would provide an excellent opportunity to enable the oriental woman, too often left out of things, to improve her condition. The only question was which means to adopt. And the answer was soon found. The priest had visited the workshops of Ramses Wissa Wassef in Harraniya and seen the amazing results obtained

1. *Bedouin girls still wear their traditional dresses with pride.*

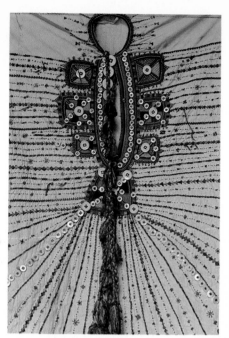

2. The black wedding dresses from the Siwa oasis are richly ornamented. The front consists of innumerable radiating lines of embroidery and mother-of-pearl buttons, simulating a sunburst.

3. On the day after her wedding, the Siwan bride wears an embroidered dress of white silk, decorated with mother-of-pearl buttons in a design of tiny suns shedding rays over the whole of the front of the dress.

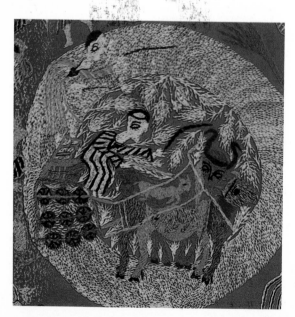

4. The embroiderers of Akhmim use an overlapping backstitch to resemble the relief effect of the old Coptic tapestries. They also sometimes adopt the motif of enclosing figures in circles to create their scenes of rural life.

5. *This young Nubian girl, working on a bead necklace, is wearing the characteristic transparent black silk dress, decorated with naïve, linear motifs representing birds and flowers, over a colorful underdress.*

6. *This Bedouin girl, from the oasis of Bahariya, is wearing the gold nose ring, gatar, an increasingly rare sight.*

7. Azza Fahmi, designer and maker of this fine modern jewelry, draws inspiration from her Egyptian heritage.

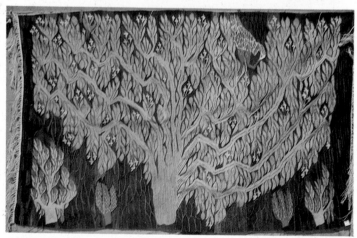

8. The tapestries of Harraniya are now famous worldwide. These 'child-creations', which emerged from the amazing experiment directed by the architect Ramses Wissa Wassef, demonstrate a consummate technical skill combined with a naïve freshness and vigorous inventiveness to create a fund of inexhaustible poetry.

11. *Weavings from Kerdasa, depicting village life, are popular with tourists.*

9. *The weavings done by the women of Garagos reproduce the designs by artists from Cairo with remarkable skill.*

10. *The deliberate choice of vivid colors in the weavings from Garagos help reflect the spirit of the Egyptian countryside.*

12. *At Nagada, in Upper Egypt, weaving has survived, thanks to the women, who use small looms to make the silk wraps called* melayas.

by the apprentices. There was nothing to prevent initiating a similar experiment.

So new recruits invaded the workshops designed by Hassan Fathy, the prestigious architect of Gurna, along the traditional lines of the buildings of Upper Egypt. Beneath the domes and arches which seem so ageless, young weavers exerted themselves at their looms. During the first stage, these young weavers in petticoats learned to weave thick-pile rugs, similar to those of Old Cairo. But the task proved difficult. It was hard work to stretch the warp threads on the looms chosen by Father Ackermann, which were inspired by primitive models. The production required an enormous amount of wool and time for a result that was sometimes mediocre. The instructor realized this, and decided to go to the famous tapestry school in Aubusson, in France, to take part in a training program with Tabard, who was master weaver there in the fifties and sixties.

Father Ackermann had just played his lucky card. In Aubusson he met the painter Jean Lurçat, who was instrumental in revolutionizing the art of tapestry, largely by limiting the choices of colors, worked with him, and succeeded in arousing his interest in the project. The famous Lurçat came to Garagos! He wanted to judge for himself and share in the experience. Won over by the vivacity and enthusiasm of the young girls, he drew some tapestry patterns for them. This made Father Ackerman change direction. The workshops of Garagos abandoned the weaving of thick-pile rugs and launched into tapestries. Very quickly the young weavers learned how to copy the patterns and make the designs on the weft.

The reputation of the weavers did not take long to spread throughout the country. Art lovers procured designs for them from paintings and tapestries, and asked them to make them. The bet was won. The women of Garagos had succeeded in opening a new window on their future.

Following this renown, an annual exhibition, held in one or another of the religious establishments of Cairo, became the link with their clientèle. But there is another side to the picture. Trained in a technique, and skillful at reproducing precisely drawn patterns, would these young girls be able to graduate from this level, and attain to creation? When Father Ackermann attempted this challenge, he ran into insurmountable barriers. His skilled trainees were incapable of originality. They were too primitive, too attached to the act of reproducing. Without a doubt, the repetition of the same act over months, if not years, had suffocated any spark of inventiveness.

However, to prevent the Garagos workshop from becoming dull or stale, Ackermann gave the weavers perfect outline drawings of the works produced by the pupils of Harraniya, as well as patterns from Egyptian painters, and Coptic motifs like those from Akhmim. It was already a boon to know that the tapestries of Garagos were preserving and reflecting the soul of Egypt.

From time to time, as the years go by, a girl does weave from inspiration, without using a pattern, to make a marvelous, imaginative tapestry. This is the proof that anything is still possible. But it did not occur during the pioneer years. For the most part, those girls achieved no more than excellent craftsmanship. Currently, a French woman is training a group of children in the technique of tapestry, giving free rein to their imaginations. We will have to wait and see what this crop yields.

In the interval, about twenty weavers, now between thirty and forty years old, gather daily to work in the studio. The tapestries which they weave, with infinite care, bear witness to an excellent technique and a very distinctive style. (See color illustrations 9 and 10.)

Kerdasa—or Tourist Crafts

From the road which leads to the famous Pyramids of Giza, you turn right to reach a village which is both geographically and qualitatively diametrically opposed to, and which in some ways competes with, Harraniya. This is Kerdasa, a very familiar name to tourists, and where every other house contains a weaving loom.

In this area, situated on the edge of arable land, and a few kilometers from the desert which separates Cairo from Alexandria, weaving is the principal activity upon which the villagers have depended for decades. The visitor who is not afraid of burrowing into the winding alleys will see old women seated cross-legged, distaff in hand, on the doorsteps of the mud houses. With rapid and precise movements, they spin the cotton and wool in the same manner as their ancestors. Other peasant women—and this is supreme progress—work with bizarre spinning 'machines', most often the product of the ingenuity of their husbands. In general they are built of pieces of wood and reeds attached to an old bicycle wheel. This is how the thread destined for the weavers is spun.

Inside the houses the spectacle is no less worthy of interest. Each member of the family has a role to play around the many and diverse types of archaic weaving looms. Strangely, all of this evokes the memory of scenes of activity in Akhmim and Nagada. Traditionally, brightly colored cotton and silk cloths criss-crossed by gold or silver thread are woven in Kerdasa. These serve to clothe the female population on feast days. Other sorts of fabrics regularly take the road to Siwa oasis, to Libya and sometimes to Sudan. The artisans also make woolen blankets and rugs on a red, ochre or green background. This production, of no great artistic value, has a well-established market, but would certainly not, by itself, have conferred on the village the prestige which it currently enjoys with the tourists! But Kerdasa took full advantage of the proximity of Harraniya and the astuteness of the three big factory owners.

At the time when the interest created by the children's weaving done in the workshops of Wissa Wassef attracted the tide of tourists towards

Harraniya, the owners of local enterprises had the idea of assigning other tasks to the weavers who hovered around them. Along with their customary work, they were taught to make tapestries using the pictures and designs taken from Wissa Wassef's catalogues. This is not a secret but, in fact, an initiative of which the village is proud.

The tapestries of Kerdasa obviously cannot withstand a comparison with those of Harraniya. The technique is not as good, the designs do not have the least spontaneity, and it is commonly admitted that a single theme may be repeated time after time. But it is also true that with this 'copying', a style of popular tapestry was born. Actually the weavers have, little by little, gained enough courage to try out their own visions: peasant houses encircled by birds, rivers with visible fish, village weddings, barnyards in turmoil, camel drivers, 'stick' dances (*tahtib*), popular cafés . . . . Because they are now reproduced in their hundreds— this being the principal reproach levelled at them—these tasteful representations of the peasant life of Egypt are now scattered to the four corners of the world. Reasonably priced, these tapestries are very affordable to tourists, an argument working in their favor. (See color illustration 11.)

In Kerdasa many weavers are connected with the three factories, or with the boutiques which now line the main street of the village. Others work for the merchants from Cairo, generally those from Khan al Khalili. Following the example of Akhmim, they make reversible bedspreads and tablecloths, while the silk and cotton fabrics woven for the foreigners are plainer and more beautiful than those destined for popular local consumption. Here, the entrepreneurial spirit has widened the scope of traditional production. We must hope that the inventive spirit will play an even greater role.

WHERE TO FIND

Akhmim Tapestries
- some state-owned stores, like Salon Vert and Hannaux in Kasr al Nil Street, downtown Cairo
- Cadeaux Chics, 4A, Hassan Assim Street, Zamalek, Cairo
- Safarkhan, 6, Brazil Street, Zamalek, Cairo
- Moquette Center, 24, Ibrahim Street, Heliopolis, Cairo, and 27, Gamat al Dawal al Arabia, Mohandiseen, Cairo
- Akhmim: the *suq*, and in the studios of weavers not associated with the Upper Egypt Association
- biennial exhibition in Cairo organized by the Upper Egypt Association (the venue is announced for each event)

Other Handwoven Tapestries

- Khan al Khalili, Cairo, for carpets, tapestries and rugs made in Kerdasa, Harraniya, the Fayoum, Beni Suef, etc.
- Kerdasa for locally produced rugs, and you can visit the studios
- stores at the Pyramids of Giza
- stores along the road to Harraniya
- *suqs* and studios of Upper Egypt (Nagada, Garagos, Sohag, Asyut)
- *suqs* of Luxor and Aswan
- stores and *suqs* in the tourist centers of Sinai (Sharm al Sheikh, Nuweiba, al Arish), and the Bedouin villages

Fine Art Tapestries

- Ramses Wissa Wassef's Center at Harraniya, outside Cairo
- Senouhi, 54, Abdel Khaleq Sarwat Street, downtown Cairo (owns exclusive rights to the tapestries produced by Ramses Wissa Wassef's Center at Harraniya
- the Weaving Center established by Father Ackermann in Garagos, or in the homes of the weavers attached to it

4

Embroidery

It is perhaps difficult to imagine that many centuries before the Christian era, workers were already laboring, needle and thread in hand, to enrich cloth with embroidery. All the same, it is true that various forms of embroidery existed in ancient Egypt. It has often been noted that pharaonic craftsmen embroidered patterns onto cloth because they did not know how to weave designs into it. A little later, during the third and fourth centuries, certain Coptic fabrics had their designs worked entirely in embroidery, especially on clothing. Later still, in Islamic Egypt, silk embroidery appeared on linen cloth.

All of this leads to a curious observation. Egyptian embroiderers, and oriental embroiderers in general, have never used their talents on tablecloths, towels or napkins. This practice is rather modern. Perhaps it can be attributed to the absence of a dining room, in the Western sense of the term. Formerly, in the Arab world, meals were put on large, round platters of silver or copper (*saniya*), low tables (*tabliya*), or even on large plates of braided straw. The diners sat around them cross-legged or on low divans.

Be that as it may, embroidery has been practiced for centuries in Egypt, and still is in some regions. It was used to decorate some male clothing, such as skullcaps and vests, but especially in the
preparation of the woman's wedding dress (see chapter 1). This is an essential activity. Each adolescent girl devotes herself to this task with wholehearted zeal, for reasons which are more sentimental than æsthetic. The quality of the embroidery will prove her manual dexterity, its richness will testify to the financial means of her father, and all of this will hasten the marriage proposals.

Formerly, each governorate had its own style of wedding dress, but this custom is being lost, the modern tendency being to have a dress made by the village seamstress. The result is that young girls today are no longer learning embroidery skills from their mothers and grandmothers, except in Sinai, at Sharqiya, in Nubia and in the oases of Kharga, Dakhla and Siwa. Usually the dress is basically black, but the bodice, the sleeves and the hemline of the dress are almost entirely covered by fine embroidery in which cross-stitch or chainstitch are combined to create ravishing geometrical and floral patterns.

Mention should be made of another development in the last few decades. This is the creation of numerous workshops operated by charity organizations, both Muslim and Christian, where girls from underprivileged backgrounds are assured of work by learning French and English styles of embroidery. Cairo, Alexandria, Port Said, Ismailia, Mansura, Tanta, Asyut, Akhmim, and dozens of other cities have such workshops. But these embroiderers, who subsequently become professional

Apprentices in the eighteenth century learning embroidery skills which they applied to cotton, linen, silk, and even leather. From Description de l'Égypte.

seamstresses, are not to be confused with the young women who embroider their own dresses in their own villages, following simple and authentic traditional styles passed down from mother to daughter.

Akhmim

In this context, unique to Egypt, Akhmim serves to exemplify what has happened in Egypt since about 1960. An ancient weaving city, where the practice of different sorts of crafts continues to absorb a good part of the local work force, Akhmim currently occupies a choice position in the artistic scene, thanks to the 'spontaneous embroidery' done by about a hundred young girls.

It all began with the arrival of two female instructors at the of Upper Egypt Association's Center for Schools and Social Development. They came to do social work, and immediately found a neglected group of people who needed help: women. In the cities and villages of Upper Egypt, even more than in the rest of the country, their condition was miserable. A woman's role consisted exclusively of subordinate, menial work, and she was barred from any form of distraction. In the street, Muslim and Christian women alike had to keep their faces veiled according to old and inexorable customs.

But sometimes it was possible to see curiosity and vivacity in the eyes peering out from under the veils, which transformed the feminine figure into dark, shapeless ghosts. These eyes were wide open and thoroughly alert. And once the instructors had gained the confidence of these women, enough to be invited into their homes, they were able to observe a fierce desire to live. These young women were no longer blindly submissive like their grandmothers. They were determined to be useful and to do something worthwhile, not only for the sake of independence, but also because they felt they had a role to play. They chose to learn to embroider, and not just on a whim. Two associations, one Muslim and the other Coptic, had already been teaching several young girls the basics of European embroidery for a few years. This initiative, which did not provoke violent male reactions, allowed them to take canvas and thread home, and to make themselves a little money, so it was worth following up. The young instructors had no objection, but they would have liked to pursue a better, more distinctive route. It was then that the past of Akhmim inspired them. This heritage was present in the five hundred weaving looms which gave life to the city. However, Akhmim owed its fame to the period of the third and fourth centuries, which saw weavers create the 'Coptic textiles'. So why have these young women, who were mostly Copts, work on European patterns? Why not link up with tradition?

This idea encouraged the teachers to come up with their own designs. It was enough to reproduce a few patterns on canvas for them to end up with all sorts of convolutions. After all, the woven textiles were distinguished by the influence of pharaonic Egypt, by Hellenistic and Persian art. The range of patterns was therefore very wide, ranging from simple inscriptions through biblical scenes, stylized flowers, circles and squares in geometric or floral patterns, to foliage inhabited by small people and animals. But to accentuate the resemblance with the past, it would be necessary to preserve the style, unique to Coptic textiles, which gives a distinctive relief, a depth, to the designs. The weavers of the early centuries possessed the secret of this special weaving technique. How could this new venture achieve the same effect in embroidery? Some research, a touch of imagination, and the instructors invented a special stitch, very simple, a sort of overlapping backstitch, which exactly reproduced the desired effect. By using it to embroider flowers and figures, they were able to achieve the rippling masses of color which are the singular hallmark of Coptic textiles.

Thrilled to be able to assert their personalities, the first recruits worked with the zeal of neophytes. They tirelessly embroidered scenes of biblical life, and each work became a veritable picture. At the end of the year an exhibition was organized in Cairo. It aroused public interest and encouragement, which just served to redouble the enthusiasm of the young women. They felt they had found the right path.

Over the years, this enthusiasm, which never lost its intensity, was combined with a sense of tangible achievement, and encouraged the instructors to experiment with original, creative embroidery. Most of the embroiderers were illiterate, but then, so were the weavers of the fourth century. There was no reason why their descendants should be any less gifted than they were.

A trial run would be made with another group of girls, younger and still inexperienced, so that, compared with the first group of young women, they were more receptive to, and less conscious of the importance of the proposed initiative. It would suffice to stir the imagination of these very sensitive beings, who felt instinctively the beauty of a rural landscape or a sunset. The instructors encouraged the girls to look more closely at the people and things around them, and to attempt to draw the images which particularly struck or attracted them. They rarely had to provide suggestions.

Without instruction in drawing, people of any age still sketch quite childishly, simply, naïvely, and often with a total lack of logic, in picturesque defiance of the laws of perspective. This is just what happened at Akhmim. Day after day, the apprentices drew cats as big as people, houses smaller than camels or donkeys. Friends and relations, their familiar environment, inspired the artists. All sorts of rural scenes would appear on the fabric, traced in chalk by unskilled hands. Whole pictures came spontaneously, colorfully and amusingly into being.

The annual exhibition encouraged and confirmed the girls' talents. Radiant, the adolescents refused to copy the Coptic patterns which had always guided their older colleagues. They wanted to embroider their own visions. Thus Akhmim, the legendary crucible of innovative handicraft, became the setting for the most interesting artistic adventure of recent years. It can be described in many ways: as a unique attempt, as the birth of a new style, and as further proof that every human being has the gift of imagination and creation when circumstances are favorable, and no exterior intervention influences its manner of expression.

Ten years on, the so-called 'spontaneous embroidery' of Akhmim has earned the right to be included in Egyptian artistic life. (See color illustration 13.) Its renown has even passed beyond the local context and reached as far as Europe and America, where exhibitions have attracted throngs of visitors in Paris, Montreal, San Francisco, Berlin, Washington, Houston, Montreal again . . . .

Fortunately, the enthusiastic attention of the public has not spoiled the talent of the young girls. They have kept their simplicity and the desire to develop and maintain an individual style. This is immediately evident on a visit to the center, an attractive building with arched windows and domed roofs. In the garden, or in the main hall, there are fifteen to twenty girls working without interruption. Some embroider while others are still at the drawing stage. The presence of visitors does not prevent them from concentrating. Each one is sitting, or standing, in front of her canvas. Chalk in hand, she sketches an outline on the fabric. A house appears, an animal, or an immense flower. If the result does not satisfy the young artist she shakes the fabric. The chalk drawing blurs and she begins again. The use of chalk allows for this reworking. One feels that there is an effort at composition and research, that the artist does not literally copy her own familiar world onto the canvas, and that she guards against being influenced by her colleagues' work. When she is happy with what she has drawn, she chooses the colored threads she wants and begins to embroider. It now becomes evident that the drawing is not a definitive tracing, but rather a general theme. Along the way, each embroiderer enriches her initial sketch with a thousand imaginative details: flowers, birds, dogs, ducks, or even small people, as inspiration dictates. What they depict in their own creations is the world which surrounds them, or the tales and legends which they have heard.

From time to time a girl or young woman arrives asking for cloth or thread. Working in the center itself is not obligatory. The majority of the embroiderers do their work at home. Indeed, this was the original goal, to give them the means to improve their social and financial condition without upsetting their way of life. Thus the center currently counts about a hundred members, but each works according to her own schedule and at her own rhythm.

Naturally, it is to be hoped that ventures like this one multiply throughout the country, since they are a way of propagating a quality handicraft while at the same time giving young people a trade.

But whatever happens, it is the pioneers of Akhmim who deserve the credit. Each year the public waits with impatience for the exhibition which will permit them to purchase tablecloths and napkins done in ravishing embroidery. But the trophy rests incontestably with the embroidered pictures. These are sometimes large compositions, landscapes or legends related with care, but mostly they consist of scenes where people and birds are often framed in circles or ovals, a modern reincarnation of the Coptic style. (See color illustration 4.) Quite often, too, the pictures overflow their frames and scatter luxuriantly over the whole cloth. Reality is swept away by a great artistic breath. Embroidered drawings in a wealth of shimmering colors confirm that cats can swim in rivers and that birds walk about on the backs of camels. Fish and dogs rub shoulders quite amicably, while miniature boats sail away on a crescent moon for a long voyage to Wonderland.

WHERE TO FIND

* Traditional embroidery is found on women's clothing (see Chapter 1).
* The 'spontaneous embroidery' pictures by the girls of Akhmim, as well as napkins, cushion covers, etc. are to be found at the biennial exhibition of their work organized in Cairo by the Upper Egypt Association (the venue is announced for each event).
* There are workrooms in quarters of Cairo (Qubba, Imbaba) attached to the Association for the Protection of Women and Children, which hold an annual exhibition, the venue of which is announced each year.
* Tahsin al Sahha Association, Sheikh Rihan Street, downtown Cairo.This workroom produces some beautiful pieces, but the embroidery is usually done by machine.
* The Social Center of the Episcopal Church at Bulaq runs a program for local women to earn money by embroidering tablecloths, napkins, cushion covers, pillowcases, etc. They are sold at various bazaars and functions throughout the year in Cairo, and at the center itself, 36 al Qalaa Street, Bulaq, Cairo.

5

Tentmaking

In a noisy and dusty quarter of Cairo, where the voice of the muezzin imposes silence and respect five times daily, a fortress gate looms up, massive and menacing. It is Bab Zuweila, the southern gate of the ancient Fatimid capital, and it has the appearance of a European castle gatehouse relocated in the Orient by mistake or miracle. Once through the gate, the sense of disorientation is further accentuated. There is no military machinery, but a long narrow street, covered by a stone ceiling and lined with minuscule shops crowded with tailors.

Behind Bab Zuweila is the province of the *khiyamiya*, those craftsmen who specialize in making tents (*khiam*), the gaudy Bedouin shelters and lodgings formerly used by princes while traveling or hunting. However, the princes have disappeared, and Bedouins nowadays have less exotic tastes. It is no longer for them that the artisans arrange vividly colored cloth, forming large arabesques and pharaonic characters, to sew by hand onto the canvas background. Now they work on special tents called *siwan*. Easy to put up and take down, they have proven their use at open-air events. Such 'marquees' constitute the largest part of the tentmakers' work, but these craftsmen also make all sorts of things to attract a modern clientèle. Seated cross-legged, scissors and needles to hand, they sew, in this honeycomb of cell-like, often windowless, workshops. It is at once strange and touching to watch them work under the protection of Bab Zuweila, in the midst of the remains of the Fatimid caliphate which was the heyday of their craft. The skillful addition of scraps of cloth, piece by colored piece, to a much larger one, in order to compose different patterns, goes back to the most ancient times. Examples of fabric decorated like this have been found in the tombs of royal families of the New Kingdom. This procedure, it is said, was one of the first known attempts at adorning fabric quickly and cheaply. In its simplest form, the technique resembles patching, which is, in fact, how certain historians describe it. But this definition is rather crude, and it masks the advantage that this decorative style provides of embellishing fabrics destined for the most diverse uses. Over the centuries, it has generally been used to make tents prettier, to the point where this fundamental activity eventually gave its name to the craft itself. The literal translation of al fann al khiami is 'the art of tentmaking'.

It is certain that these cloth shelters have been fashionable in Egypt since the pharaonic era. To protect himself from the sun while traveling up and down the Nile, a pharaoh had an umbrella-shaped tent erected on his boat. For his journeys on land he possessed some very luxurious ones. But it is particularly in the time of the Fatimid caliphs that the tents became decorated with floral and animal designs, so similar to those made today. These caliphs lived a life of luxury and ostentation, and did not expect to live any less self-indulgently while moving from place to place. So to spare him from having to endure less comfortable living conditions, the practice grew of transforming his tent into a veritable 'mobile palace'. For the sake of æsthetics, the ornate and precious furniture which was put in the various rooms—reception room, council hall, and bedroom—had to be set off by equally sumptuously decorated walls. Thus the practice was developed of embellishing the bare canvas with colorful designs, made using the technique rather derogatively called 'patching'—perhaps more accurately called 'appliqué'—since embroidery would have required a superhuman effort. The craftsmen who developed this art form saw their golden age in the tenth century.

Following this, the Ayyubid dynasty adopted the same customs. In addition, princely wedding ceremonies took place in the famous 'marriage tent', for which the preparation required nine years of work from the artisans. At one time, the sultans also decided to erect beautiful reproductions of this type in some cities and to reside there from time to time. Rather as one goes camping for a change of air.

From one decade to the next, these tents, decorated in arabesques, and initially conceived for hunting and traveling, proved useful for all sorts of ceremonies. This is the very use they are put to today, so establishing a marvelous continuity through history, since in the end nothing has changed, not the technique, nor the style of decoration, nor the social and religious function of these transitory lodgings.

Under his skillful fingers, the arabesques are created perfectly and exactly, and with stupefying speed. Photograph: Hassan Hamed

The primary function of the siwan is to receive the people who come to present their condolences after a funeral.

The artisans gathered in the tentmakers' bazaar, the Khiyamiya in Cairo, continue to work just like their ancestors—to the extent that if it were not for the neon lights illuminating the workshops, you would think you were on a pilgrimage to the past. Seeing them busy at their work, it is clear that it is a shared craft. It is usually the father of the family who draws or marks the chosen design on the background canvas. His inspiration may be drawn from the wall decoration of a mosque or simply from a book of Islamic art. This is why he traces lotus flowers reminiscent of pharaonic designs, stylized flowers, elegant combinations of circles and triangles, interlaced foliations, and graceful arabesques. Actually, the square and rectangular canvas panels offer little variety. When the master craftsman has finished his design, his collaborators, most often his children or younger brothers, cut and arrange according to the design, the strips of black, yellow, red, blue, green or orange fabric. They will apply themselves to sewing them, using a simple invisible stitch, like that used for making a hem. The finished panels will be fitted together, and end up forming the sides of the great rectangular tents called *siwan*, the use of which has nowadays spread throughout Egypt.

This is an easily observed fact. The *siwan* are set up in Cairo, as in all of the cities and villages of the country, to shelter participants at any kind of open-air gathering, be it a religious ceremony, engagement or wedding party, cocktail party, or even a press conference or a speech given by the President of the Republic. But the primary function of the *siwan* is to receive the people who come to present their condolences after a funeral. Just this short list shows how varied is the use of the same tents, even the same motifs, which serve as the decor of ceremonies of fundamentally differing characters. However, this does not bother the artisans, who are quite unable to justify the contradiction. They only know how to handle their needles. Under their skillful fingers, the arabesques are created perfectly and exactly, and with stupefying speed. They also make tents for pilgrims going to Mecca, mostly for a Saudi clientèle, but this work has a more sober character, employing designs using only green and black, the colors of the Prophet. Another use of the fabrics which they prepare is to decorate the streets of the big cities for official occasions or holidays.

It can be said that today, thanks to the *siwan*, an ancient tradition is being kept alive. The past also lives again through another interesting belief; Bab Zuweila is often nicknamed 'Bab al Metwalli' because a very pious man, Qutb al Metwalli, once lived there. The old artisans claim that his spirit used to come back to the quarter, and that a glimmer of light revealed his presence. This glimmer no longer appears, but the sick still come occasionally and pin shreds of cloth, which have touched their bodies, to the bronze nails of the door, in the hope of being healed. The presence of these supplicants offers a complete contrast to the regulars of Bab Zuweila: the businessmen of Cairo and elsewhere who come to deliver an order, and the waves of talkative tourists.

It is they, the tourists, who instigated and encouraged a new application of *al fann al khiami*. Every day they came in small groups, unrestrained in their enthusiasm. They admired the majestic gate, the voice of the muezzin and the work of the artisans. They fingered the material, asked questions, and lingered to talk. It was perfectly obvious that they would have loved to make a few purchases. But it is not every day that one needs a tent, and how would one carry it home by plane? What is certain is that their regular visits and the interest which they manifested were the fundamental cause of the transformation of this craft. In response to the wishes of this foreign clientèle, as warm as it was unexpected, the artisans, following the advice of the merchants, partially modified their production, in order to give it a touristic character. Along with tentmaking, the work which guaranteed their survival, they adapted the technique of *al fann al khiami* to pieces which would easily find a place in a European or American interior. They quickly came up with items that could serve as tablecloths, napkins, cushion covers or wall hangings. Just recently, the artisans have expanded their work into using their designs on bags, dresses and evening wear.

To attract tourists, the tentmakers have adapted their work to make cushion covers, wall hangings, etc.

This last stage promises to be the most advantageous, but it also risks dealing a fatal blow to the purity and authenticity of this craft. Particularly so, because, as the *khiyamiya* work for this foreign clientèle, they no longer keep to their traditional designs. They realized quite rapidly that pharaonic or folkloric scenes reproduced on a wall hanging or a cushion cover sell very quickly, and they have not hesitated to adapt to these styles. It was easy for them to draw from the illustrations in history books. Taking up the most famous scenes, or the most striking faces, they sketched solar boats, dancing girls, pharaohs seated on their thrones, and the four sons of Horus. Other designs include a succession of solemn pharaohs frozen in eternal poses, the superb Nefertiti, or the god–kings with mysterious faces, Anubis, the funerary god with the head of a jackal, the *khepri-scarab* who personifies the rising sun, or monstrous Taweret, the goddess with the body of a hippopotamus and the feet of a lion. The most amusing part is that the craftsman arranges these pharaohs at his own whim, without the least concern for historical chronology, and so comes up with scenes that would make an Egyptologist despair.

The second theme in use is Egyptian peasant life. Its exoticism seduces foreigners, thus inspiring the workers of Bab Zuweila to portray peasants smoking waterpipes (*goza*), dancers, riders on horses or camels, huts leaning against palm trees, peasant women carrying *balalis* on their heads; in fact, the entire imagery of the average tourist, everything which represents Egypt in his eyes is depicted in a startling array of vivid colors.

In short, this last decade has improved the condition of the artisans at the price of a rather serious concession. In playing to the tourists' taste, *al fann al khiami* has certainly lost some of its authenticity. What is happening is unfortunately not a rejuvenation of the craft but a corruption. This danger is made all the more serious by a local development that will threaten the craft sooner or later. Recently, factories have been producing fabrics decorated with traditional patterns. Printing has begun to replace appliqué and could even supersede it. A *siwan* of printed canvas costs much less than a tent made by hand. Already, *siwans* whose printed lengths have been skillfully mixed with sections constructed in appliqué can be seen in the streets of Cairo. This is the first step. The second consists of going only to the factories. The artisans gloomily resent this state of affairs, which might deprive them of their livelihood in the years to come. They would then have to resign themselves to changing their profession, or to working only for the tourists. In either case, the craftsmen are going to suffer.

WHERE TO FIND

- the Khiyamiya, near Bab Zuweila, Cairo (for sale and to order)
- Khan al Khalili, for cushion covers, bags, wall hangings, etc.
- Mamelouk, 4A, Hassan Assim Street, Zamalek, Cairo

- Kerdasa
- stores near the Pyramids of Giza
- stores on the road to Harraniya
- shopping centers in the large hotels in Cairo
- *suqs* of Luxor and Aswan

6

Leather

Renowned as weavers, basketmakers, and potters since the earliest of times, Egyptians have never been able to forge a reputation in leatherwork. This deficiency has a very simple explanation. Egypt has no history of animal husbandry; the rearing of sheep or goats, buffalo or cattle, was not known even during the pharaonic dynasties. The peasants of the early centuries, like those of the twentieth century, kept, at most, enough livestock to enable them to work their land, with a resultant limited supply of leather. The artisans were content to make only those things of prime importance: sandals, belts, water-bags, containers for storing butter or cheese, and a very large leather bottle called a *saqqa*, capable of holding an entire family's water supply. There was never any question of exporting these products, which naturally precluded any international reputation.

In the beginning of Islam, Egyptians were able to cover their copies of the Koran in very fine bindings, but this state of affairs seems to have been rather short-lived. No especially good specimens have ever been found, and we cannot justifiably speak of a tradition—although it is, occasionally, just these sorts of circumstances which favor a form of handicraft. In the last centuries, with Egypt being an obligatory stop for

African pilgrims going to Mecca, the artisans specialized in making the leather sandals so indispensable to travelers. According to custom, every prospective *hagg* (the title given to a person who has completed the holy pilgrimage) must wear sandals made with nails, not sewn with any thread at all. Also, with pilgrims in mind, large studded belts, which in reality serve as money belts, are made. The richer the pilgrim, the fancier the belt, decorated with additional studs and extra leather. But these are exceptions. Actually, the scarcity of leather was so great, that Mohammed Ali, at the time he wanted to outfit his army, had to obtain leather from Bulgaria. The word *bulgha*, denoting the popular style of shoes, is derived from *Bulgharya*, the Arabic name for Bulgaria.

All of this proves that leather crafts, as we know them now, are of recent origin. Principally conceived for tourists, the craft is centered around the famous Khan al Khalili, Cairo's tourist center.

It is immediately obvious that the tanneries are not located in the neighborhood of the *suq*. The cutting and tanning of the hides requires space and sun for the many operations. The tanners have thus established their workshops in less crowded areas: Masr al Qadima, Sayeda Zeinab and Ain al Sira, that is, round Old Cairo and the ancient Fatimid capital of Fustat. It is there that tanners can be seen at work, pinning the hides to wide, wooden panels fixed on the sidewalks, or engaged in all sorts of preparations inside their workshops, which are not much more than dark and gloomy sheds. Tanning is done with the help of vegetable and chemical substances, as is the coloring of the skins. Other large cities like Alexandria or Tanta also have tanneries, but the majority of the actual leatherworkers, those who make the items for sale, work in the capital, particularly in the shops bordering Khan al Khalili. They form a sort of ring around the merchants, some of whom are also the proprietors of the workshops. And it is the merchants who make all the business transactions, from the buying of the hides to the sale of the finished product.

The assortment of skins available in Egypt is quite broad: calf, cow, goat, sheep, buffalo, camel, and even crocodile, lizard, and snake, imported from Sudan, and sometimes from Kenya. Perfectly tanned and carefully dyed, these skins constitute excellent material for a craftsman's hands to work on. It would be wonderful if they really applied themselves to making the best use of their skills and material, but this is rarely the case. Paid by the piece, the artisan is obliged to produce quickly in order to survive. This is not an incentive for creativity. Each of them simply strives to make the greatest number of objects in the minimum amount of time. Not one shows any desire to improve his production and bring it up to date. This sad fact is immediately evident on a visit to the workshops.

First of all, it is clear that specialization reigns as absolute master. The artisan who makes the circular hassocks (pouffes) does not waste his time sewing bags. The one who braids belts undertakes no other task. The craft can only just be classed as semiskilled. In this respect, the most disappointing fact is perhaps that none of the workmen regrets the introduction of the sewing machine for joining the pieces of leather, or the use of heat-stamps for printing patterns on the various items. In their eyes, this is progress from which they can benefit. Imaginative effort and detailed work occupy only a minimal place in their daily lives.

But the absence of a professional pride among these artisans does not mean that they lack skill. Here too, the marvelous dexterity, so widespread in Egypt, is present. In the workshops where hassocks are made, for example, expert hands cut diamond shapes in black, red, yellow, green, brown or gray, arrange them to make a regular pattern, then sew them by machine; only the outside edge, which tidies all the seams into the inside, is done by hand. The hassocks are then decorated with pharaonic or Islamic patterns. Those which show up most frequently are the faces of Nefertiti or Ramses II, pharaonic scenes, dancing girls, musicians, horsemen, princes wearing majestic turbans, and Koranic verses. These same patterns are found on all of the objects from purses to jewelry boxes, because they are simply prints which are heat-stamped onto the leather. In fairness, it should be mentioned that occasionally a craftsman can be seen cutting decorative geometric designs into leather using a sharp wooden stylus. Other leatherworkers have recently decided to adapt the appliqué techniques of the *khiyamiya* (the tentmakers) to leather crafts. Just like their colleagues who work with cloth (see chapter 5), they cut strips of colored leather, then attach them to the plain surface of a hassock or purse to create floral and geometric patterns, and even small scenes of peasant life. They fix them either by machine-sewing them, or with glue, which looks neater, but is less secure. The results are very pretty, and tourists are greatly attracted by them. Unfortunately, however, this creative effort has not been adopted by the majority of the artisans who continue to work, ceaselessly, and without question, day after day repeating the same work over and over again.

In workshop after workshop, they make hassocks, wallets, handbags, and jewelry boxes . . . . There are no surprises, since the process of production always follows the same pattern. It could truthfully be said that the production methods in leathercraft have not varied for decades, and that a well-supplied shop is representative of just about all that is made in Cairo. There it all is, carefully arranged on shelves: cigarette and jewelry boxes, pencil cases, sheaths for knives, wallets and billfolds, purses and holdalls of leather, lizard skin or crocodile skin, book covers, frames, desk sets and desk tidies containing everything from card holders to writing pads. In one corner of the store, the hassocks are piled up, while strings of sandals and slippers (*babush*) hang in garlands from the ceiling. There are also short colonial-style riding crops, fly-swatters, and innumerable colored camels of different sizes, which could serve either as toys or trinkets.

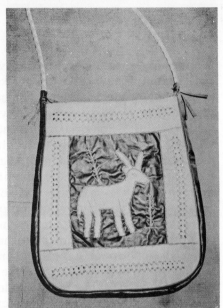

top left *A hassock decorated with the same heat-stamped pharaonic or Islamic patterns that are found on all the objects made in leather.*

top right *A bag decorated with pieces of leather sewn on to create a scene of peasant life.*

bottom *Strings of slippers (babush) hang in garlands from the ceilings of leathergoods stores.*

Photographs: Denise Ammoun

Certainly it is all very attractive to the tourist. But from a purely artistic angle, leathercrafts are stuck in a rut. Throughout the whole craft, there is no whisper of originality discernible, no complicated technique, no minutely worked patterns. Sadly, the same has to be said of the workshops of Alexandria and Asyut which turn out very similar pieces—and those only in the cases where the merchants do not come to Cairo for their wares, as do the traders of Suez, Port Said, and Ismailia.

In a few regions, there are little islands of artistry, which have escaped from this banality and still demonstrate a creativity which is both authentic and interesting. Unfortunately, their work is not offered to the wider public. In many Coptic convents, monks and nuns make a variety of very skillfully braided leather crosses. And in the village of Hawawish in Upper Egypt, and in several villages along the range of mountains on both sides of the Nile valley, there are still some artisans to be found who make magnificent saddles for horses and camels—so keeping alive some of the poetry of the desert. Here speed of production is not an important factor. All that is required is a love for the work. Similarly, in the oases of Kharga and Dakhla, but for the local market only, they still make lovely, stylish Bedouin clogs in different colored leathers.

These objects, which have a real charm, are not for sale to the general public. From a strictly commercial perspective, this makes no difference to the current economic context, because leathercrafts are doing well enough as they are. Production is rapid, as is turnover. Expecting the exotic, and seduced by the magic of the Orient, tourists overlook the poor quality of the work as they plunge headlong into a maze of oriental-cum-pharaonic hassocks and slippers.

WHERE TO FIND

- Khan al Khalili and the studios around it
- stores in the 'Commercial Passage', al Mumarr al Tugari, downtown Cairo
- shopping centers in the large hotels in Cairo
- small crafts stores in Kasr al Nil Street and Abdel Khaleq Sarwat Street, downtown Cairo
- Kerdasa
- stores on the road to Harraniya
- stores at the Pyramids of Giza
- suqs of Luxor and Aswan, and shopping centers in the large hotels
- suqs in the tourist centers of Sinai (Sharm al Sheikh, Nuweiba, al Arish)
- al Hammam, west of Alexandria, for leather shoes embroidered in silk

7

Basketry

It is said in Egypt that there are basketweavers wherever there are palm trees, which is to say that they are everywhere. Like pottery, basketry has always been a thriving trade, and both handicrafts have been present in the region for a very long time. The earliest known examples of basketweaving were found in the Fayoum.

These ancient specimens are the mats which carpeted the wheat pits. They were made using the 'columbine' technique, which is based on making a sort of continuous twisted cord out of the material, with an envelope, or end-band, often of the same material. Once tied off, these cords are coiled together into a spiral to make the desired form, each cord in turn being sewn to its neighbor. As well as these straw mats, lids and dishes of this coiled basketry have also been found in the Fayoum.

It is very easy to learn how baskets were made in the time of the pharaohs, because there are several displays of basketry, from a five-thousand-year period, in the Egyptian Museum in Cairo. There are many baskets with handles and lids, a whole series of platters, some with red or blue lines running through them, tiny colored baskets resembling candy boxes, even chairs and stools. The quality of the work commands admiration. The techniques used previously, and still used today, reveal exceptionally gifted artists. What is more, one might be tempted to label as 'modern' the shapes of the baskets, for they are exactly like those found today in the stores of Cairo and the markets of the big cities. This indicates an incredible continuity, which seems to have experienced no interruption.

Nowadays, basketweaving is practiced all over Egypt. Just as palm trees, reeds and grain crops are an integral part of the Egyptian peasants' landscape, basketry objects are a natural product of their surroundings, and are indispensable to their daily lives.

The *fellah* transports his grain in large, supple, two-handled baskets (*quffa*), which are usually made of straw in the villages, and of palm fronds in the oases. The *quffa*, with the exception of some deliberately colorful and folkloric models, do not belong to the tourist trade. The same is true of the reed baskets (*sabat*), which come in a variety of sizes, and are vaguely conical in shape. These are also currently used both in the villages and the cities. It would be difficult to find a single Egyptian household which did not possess at least one basket of this type.

All sorts of mats are also a common possession in the country. The most rudimentary type is that made in the villages on the eve of certain harvests, especially the cotton harvest. The basketmakers braid mats, called *kibs*, from reed stalks, held in place by a continuous coarse string. Peasant women sit on these mats as, with infinite patience, they clean the cotton. At the end of this task, the bales of cotton are placed on these same mats to await their sale to the government. Each peasant also owns several mats of braided straw (*hasira*), a sort of multi-purpose rug. The *fellah* sits, works, eats and sleeps on his *hasira*.

What is interesting is that the production of this kind of mat has not varied for thousands of years. The method relies principally on the skill of the craftsman. It consists of a simple braiding, the reed stalks being tied together with straw or light twine. The second technique, more complicated, involves the use of a kind of rudimentary loom, roughly approximating that used in weaving. But there is no support-frame, and the basketweaver works directly on the ground with his two bars of wood and warp threads of hemp or linen.

The *hasira* ordinarily has a background of natural straw color, embellished with red, green, orange, or blue stripes. Black rarely appears. These colors have been popular since the times of the pharaohs. The mats are decorated with geometric or floral patterns and sometimes a band of Kufic script wishing its owner happiness (*al saada*) or guaranteeing him good luck (*baraka*). Even writing short, humorous proverbs is not excluded. Mats of the same style, but of smaller dimensions, serve for prayers. All families have them, since the pious Muslim should pray five times a day, and in any case, the use of the *hasira* is not exclusive to any one religion. They are used to cover the floors of Coptic churches as well as mosques, not to mention the monasteries of Wadi Natrun.

Matmakers in the eighteenth century at work on a large hasira.
From Description de l'Egypte.

Neighbors work together on a hasira, *turning work into a pleasurable gossip session.*

However, there are places reputed for the manufacture of mats, to the extent that a village of the Sharqiya governorate was baptized 'Kafr al Hosr', that is, the 'village of mats'. Located about sixty kilometers from Cairo, it is a village of basketweavers. Essentially they make mats of all colors and sizes, but also various types of baskets for different purposes, and large, round plates (*tabaq*), all in varied designs. Although the objects made show no particular or individual style, the sight of the craftsmen at the open doorways of their houses, busy with their tools and material, is peculiar to the village. Opposite the entrance to each house, as well as in corners of the central room, are piled great heaps of palm leaves and bundles of reeds. In spite of the agricultural richness of the region, basketweaving is the principal source of revenue for each household. For once, the peasant of the Delta is a craftsman first and a farmer second, an exception which must surely be encouraged.

The *hasira* is used all over Egypt. It is an integral element of all peasant and working-class interiors, no matter how poor the household is. Middle-class households possess them too, but only out of practical necessity. In their eyes, the ownership of a real rug, of pure wool or mixed fibers, means upward social mobility. The result of this is that the average white-collar employee, a clerk or middle-level government official, is keen to exchange his *hasira* for a 'real' rug, even a mediocre one, especially if he has daughters to marry off.

Functional baskets for village use are evidently not those which are sold in the commercial markets. The former are made in particular regions, mainly in the Fayoum, but also in Upper Egypt, Nubia, and above all, in the oases. The closer you get to these regions, the more varied and elaborate the range of baskets becomes. Even the commonly used things—*quffa, sabat* or *hasira*—are better made. This is for a variety of reasons, including the skill of the basketmakers, and the number of palm trees which adorn the landscape and provide the craftsmen with a rich choice of materials. Perhaps it is also because in these regions a large part of the work is done by the women. In the villages where basketweaving is the principal means of making a living, peasant women can be seen sitting cross-legged at the thresholds of their houses, braiding baskets with amazing dexterity. Neighbors weave in groups, transforming the hours of work into pleasurable gossip sessions, a custom which in no way compromises the excellent results. The men are more discreet. They make large mats with the help of one or several of their sons, but they only speak to issue terse commands.

In the Fayoum, in Upper Egypt and in New Nubia, the working pattern is the same, with few variations. And the same can be said, too, of the baskets they all produce. These include the usual objects, indispensable to the daily life of the peasant, but also destined for the great markets of the country: Cairo, Alexandria, Asyut, Luxor, and Aswan. So, as well as the basic items (mats, baskets, and so on), another large range of objects, decorated with geometric patterns in bright colors, is produced: sewing

In the oases, basketry skills are learned from a very early age, passed on as a natural inheritance.

baskets, bread baskets, all sorts of lidded baskets, candy boxes, small beach mats, bags, hats, baskets of every size and description. Also in these regions, the large round trays (*tabaqs*) are made out of straw or of palm fronds, usually decorated in floral patterns in harmonious colors. Highly prized throughout Egypt, these trays are sometimes hung on walls as a decoration. But for centuries they have been, and still are, used as tables. It is the Arab custom to put food on a very low table (*tabliya*) around which people then sit on cushions or mats. Sometimes the *tabaq* replaces the *tabliya*, especially in the villages.

The craftsmen of the oases make exactly the same objects, but somehow give them a style that raises them onto a different plane. It is an enigma. What gives these baskets their quality? Is it the sun of the oases, a special gift, or a certain way of looking at the world? How can it be explained that in Kharga, Dakhla, and Siwa, basketweaving has achieved such a high standard, it amounts almost to a different dimension? The artisans of these places render simple palm-leaf baskets with such taste and such a perfect blending of colors, that their work often has to be considered as art. Mats and straw baskets can also testify to their

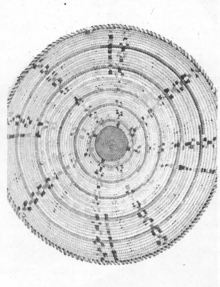

Baskets just like this can be seen in the Egyptian Museum.

Highly prized throughout Egypt, tabaqs like this are frequently hung on the wall as decoration.

makers' sense of beauty. Each item is a poem of gay colors and exquisite craftsmanship. The braiding of certain containers is, at times, so fine that it can safely hold liquid, without leaking a drop

Although the production of the oases is now largely commercial, thanks to the tourism boom, traditional work has not lost its place. There is a very picturesque matrimonial custom which persists in Dakhla. The newly married couple is given a pair of special mats especially for the wedding night. They are both oval, very colorful for the bride (bursh al arusa), and more sober for the groom (bursh al aris). A little further away, in Kharga oasis, there are still some craftsmen who know how to make clothes chests from palm fronds, but this skill is disappearing, because it is so much easier to make a chest out of wood!

As an offshoot from pure basketweaving, some artisans in Cairo, Alexandria, and Tanta specialize in the fabrication of furniture made of palm stalks. In just a few minutes they can strip the stalks, bend them, assemble them, and nail them together. With incredible speed they can make objects as varied as bird cages or flower baskets, tables or armchairs, sofas, stools, or small bars. The basic shapes are all very similar, so the craftsman can work almost without thinking, automatically, contentedly repeating the same movements indefinitely. This very repetition is the cause of an unsought bonus, in that it has given birth to a particular style, which has achieved a certain cachet and renown. The palm-stalk furniture, with its criss-cross pattern woven into the backs, and its rustic simplicity, has a character all its own. It is also undeniably solid. Sometimes, but far more rarely, this same range of furniture is made of varnished cane.

In short, although Egyptian basketweaving may not demonstrate enormous variety, the basketmakers themselves are sure to survive the progressive industrialization of the country. After all, their work consists of preparing mats and baskets for three-fourths of the population, which amounts to a guaranteed clientèle of about thirty million people. On top of this colossal market is the one catering to the tourists. This surely provides for a better future than any life-insurance plan.

This kind of craft has experienced no interruption over the course of ages. The trade continues to be passed on from father to son, from mother to daughter, with no secrets or mysteries involved. It is a natural inheritance. Children imitate what they have seen done. From infancy, they have helped with the preparation of straw stalks and palm strips, work done as a family, which means that basketweaving in Egypt remains what it has always been. It is impossible not to be conscious of a sense of ageless continuity. Adults and children work on and with the 'columbine' mats and the braided baskets, exactly as the peasants of the Nile Valley did thousands of years ago.

WHERE TO FIND

Cairo
- street-vendors in the neighborhood of 26th July Street, Zamalek
- street-vendors in the neighborhood of Baghdad Street, Heliopolis
- *hasiras* can be found in Sayeda Zeinab, and near the Ibn Tulun mosque
- palm-stalk furniture can be found in various stores in Cairo, along the road to Heliopolis, and in Heliopolis

Upper Egypt
- *suqs* of Asyut, or in the homes of the basketweavers
- *suqs* of Luxor
- *suqs* of Aswan, especially the Nubian *suq*
- homes of the basketweavers in all the villages

In the Oases
- small stores and the homes of the basketweavers in the New Valley (Kharga, Dakhla, Bahariya, Farafra) for all sorts of baskets
- small stores and the homes of the basketweavers in Siwa for the best baskets of all
- street-vendors in the Fayoum

8

Pottery

A familiar sight in Egypt is that of *feluccas* and *dahabiyas*, loaded with small mountains of pottery, slowly descending the Nile. They proceed serenely, indifferent to time or the need to hurry. And their cargo of pottery, one of the oldest forms of handicraft in the world, exudes an aura of timelessness, oblivious to the preoccupations of modern life.

An ancient craft, still heavily steeped in custom, pottery is made—more or less successfully—all across Egypt. (See color illustration 14.) On first impression, it would be easy to convince oneself that nothing has changed. The potter, albeit with the advantage of others' experiences, uses the same material as in the past, and still works a wheel which is just as primitive as that of his pharaonic colleague's. But there the comparison ends. The potters of the past were more artist than artisan. Those of our time, apart from rare exceptions, are more artisan than artist. This is easily substantiated. Consider the huge quantities of beautifully made amulets, jewelry, scarabs, and earthenware vases that have been found in the tombs of the pharaohs of antiquity. Consider, too, the ceramics made in the first centuries of Islam. During this period, potters developed and spread the secrets of making their earthenware, with its distinctive metallic glaze and inscriptive, floral, and animal motifs.

During the Fatimid era, a Persian traveler, Nasiri Khosrau, wrote: "In Egypt they make earthenware of all kinds; some so fine and translucent that one can see, through the sides of a vase, a hand laid on the exterior. They make bowls, cups, plates and other utensils. They decorate them with colors whose tones change according to the positioning of the piece." This work was done in Fustat, Old Cairo, nicknamed the 'city of pottery'. Today, examples of work once made regularly there, like the filters inserted in the necks of drinking vessels (*shubak al qulla*), fashioned like fine lace in designs of tiny birds, are shared out between museums.

But craftsmanship of that quality is now long past. In the Egypt of the twentieth century, pottery has an essentially utilitarian character. In spite of the progressive industrialization of the country, this form of handicraft continues to suppy a vital need. This is for various reasons, among which is underdevelopment. The peasants and the working classes of the cities use pottery vessels for drinking, eating, cooking, and for storing their stocks of grain and provisions of cooking oil and cheese. As a result, potters are to be found everywhere, but especially in Upper Egypt which, thanks to its clay-rich soil, holds a monopoly in mass production.

Fustat

It is easy to see potters at work. They are to be found in the populous quarters of Cairo and Alexandria, in towns and in villages. But Fustat is still the place to visit, where potters are still active, the smoke from their kilns sometimes enveloping the houses in the neighborhood. They are there, as in former times, as interdependent as ever and as devoted to their task, even though the quality of their artistry has diminished, because of socioeconomic reasons beyond their control.

Faithful to the image to which tourists are partial, the craftsmen of Fustat throw their pots in workshops with earthen floors, and walls made of reeds interwoven with palm fronds to protect them from the sun and excessive heat. They are surrounded by clay, pieces of pottery, their child–apprentices, and the curious who come to watch. Each potter is a specialist in one form of pottery. One makes little water jugs, another makes pitchers . . . , and the wheels (*dulab, agala* or *hagar*) turn ceaselessly.

Welcoming to both tourists and the serious student, the potters, like all Egyptian craftsmen, are delighted to work to an audience. They all have their stocks of raw clay beside them, and their rough and skillful fingers transform it, as they dominate both wheel and each dollop of clay. Their explanations are expansive, and they speak without stopping work. Shapes are born, at rapid and regular intervals. One makes a water jug (*qulla*), another a pitcher (*ibriq*), others produce plates (*sahn*), cooking pots (*qidra*), coffeepots (*kanaka*), vases, bowls (*sultaniya*), or flowerpots. To the casual spectator they work with dazzling speed, each lining up his

Pottery is an ancient craft, and the skills of today's potters have been refined over years of tradition.

Dahabiyas *and* feluccas *laden with pottery are a familiar sight in Egypt.*

The potter's rough and skillful fingers transform the raw clay.

Upper Egypt, thanks to its clay-rich soil, holds a monopoly in mass production.

products next to him. From time to time, each stops, wipes the sweat from his forehead, takes a large gulp from the *qulla* set at his feet, then carefully arranges his pottery in a sunny spot.

These scenes in open-air workshops, where the display and the commentary are free and generous, are to be found all over the country. With a bit of luck you will see a curiously shaped piece of pottery, widespread in Egypt, called *qullet al subua*, which translates literally as the 'vessel of the seventh day'. The parents of a newborn, boy or girl, buy it one week after the birth. Equipped with seven spouts, one for each day, it will be decorated with seven candles lit in the midst of the general happiness. Since the child has survived for seven days, he or she will live. It is an occasion to have a little party. The ritual is well-observed, being one of the most tenaciously held to in popular superstition, though it is obvious that in very large families, the joy is less ebullient after about the tenth child.

The ceremony is organized around a water jug (feminine symbol) if it is a girl, or a pitcher (masculine symbol) if it is a boy. Decorated with blue beads, very effective against the evil eye, the pitcher or water jug is filled with red and white flowers, and put on a giant platter. The number seven retains its magical significance, so seven different species of seed are set on the tray. They are usually grains of wheat, chickpeas, seeds of fenugreek, clover, and beans mixed with a few coins. When the preparations are complete, all the members of the family, each carrying a lit candle, circle the jug, led by the eldest who throws large handfuls of salt, while singing an appropriate refrain. Over the following days, the grains begin to germinate. They represent fertility, prosperity and growth.

Sometimes, to commemorate the 'seventh day', a special doll, carrying a jar (*ballas*) on her head and a seven-branched candelabrum around her waist, is bought. This doll symbolizes the traditional dances of feast days. Until the beginning of this century, peasant women who could dance without spilling a single drop of water from jars balanced on their heads, or even, incredibly, skip about with candelabra which one would have sworn were fastened to their hair, could still be found. These famous dances, which are no longer performed by more than a very few women, are kept alive through these pottery dolls. Similarly, the 'doll for the Prophet's birthday' (*aruset al mulid*) is sold in the bazaars every year.

These are not the only references to the past. The potters sometimes like to put aside their traditional work to model a horse, a cockerel, a camel or a hoopoe. In these, too, each piece of pottery has a precise significance. Throughout history the song of the cockerel has evoked the dawn prayer, and the horse has been 'man's best friend', used as a mount for his daily activities, as well as for war and hunting. The camel will not let him down: it is the inseparable companion of the Bedouin, carrying the new bride on her wedding day, enabling the Bedouin to escape from the rigors of the desert, by giving him a means of transport, nourishment from

In the past, peasant women even danced with water-pots on their heads.

In Qena, a still, silent ocean of zirs waits, under palm trees standing like guards, to be loaded onto feluccas.

its rich and thirst-quenching milk, and later, shelter, when its hair will be used for tentmaking. As for the hoopoe, its significance as the prophet Suliman's messenger demonstrates its importance. One could cite many more examples. Many links bind the twentieth century to the fundamentals of popular tradition. These are the patterns which can also be found in weaving, embroidery, and in rarer instances, in the *hassiras* of the *fellahin*.

In Egypt, you meet potters by the thousands. All day long they make jugs, pitchers, cooking pots, and bowls. These products, which do not go beyond the utilitarian, have a style which is not modified in any impressive way from one region to another; here jugs are narrower, there the pitchers have larger bellies. These variations in form could be compared with village dialects, which sometimes differ from each other for no known precise reason.

Women's role in all this is minimal. Although the first pots ever made are attributed to them, it cannot be said that Egypt boasts many woman potters. In Upper Egypt, occasionally, you see a peasant woman kneading and modeling clay with her hands, making small things like bowls, plates and cups—because she is unable to use the wheel.

Upper Egypt

Upper Egypt deserves particular attention, since the nature of its soil has made it the traditional center for pottery. But it would be pointless to visit every potter in the Said. Rather, we should spend time in the towns and cities, which bear witness to a certain specialization. In and around Qena, for example, are the potters expert in the art of making the immense jars, called *zir*, which are so absolutely peculiar to Egypt.

The *zir* guarantees the survival of all regions which as yet have no drinkable water. It is a very large piece of pottery, a sort of giant jar without handles which provides the twofold advantage of cooling and filtering water, thanks to the porous nature of the material it is made of. This consists of clay mixed with esparto grass ash. The *zir* occupies an important place in the life of rural Egypt. It is seen not only inside the squat houses, but also scattered here and there along the ribbons of road which connect the towns of Upper Egypt. Covered by a wooden board and equipped with a cup, the *zir* enables peasants and travelers to quench their thirsts. It corresponds to a law of hospitality, and is somewhat the equivalent of the drinking fountain in the West .

Making a *zir* is not a simple undertaking! Skill is necessary, and so is great physical strength. It involves turning an enormous wheel while huge quantities of clay are shaped. It is, in fact, a family activity, collective work. Each family member has a job to do, from the children who knead the clay with their feet, to the potters who take turns at the wheel, and including the adolescents who carefully transport, to a bare, sun-baked

The potter uses his whole body to make a zir.

area, the new, damp jars, which wait, lined up neatly side by side in orderly and very beautiful formation, for the weekly firing.

The governorate of Qena, and the outskirts of the city itself, are home to dozens of kilns, each surrounded by a truly infernal activity. But the most beautiful image which one retains of this area is that of a still, silent ocean of jars, waiting, under palm trees standing like guards, to be loaded onto feluccas.

The second important center is farther south, beyond Qena, on the road which leads to Luxor. Ballas is a village of potters, and a name which is used constantly by Egyptians, many of whom probably do not know its origin. For it is at Ballas, where for such a long time, and in such large quantities, that potters have been making the famous *ballas*, the indispensable jugs in daily use, which bear the name of the village they come from. It is the *ballas* which the peasant women place on their heads when they go to draw water from the river. They also use them for storing their stocks of grain, oil, cheese and honey.

Seeing how the inhabitants of Ballas center their existence on pottery, it would be easy to assume that it might very well be a special case, but many other villages can be found in Upper Egypt, where entire families base their daily activity around the making of *qullas* and *zirs*. When you watch the young boys mixing and cleaning the clay, then turn to follow attentively the work of their elders at the wheel, you realize that a full apprenticeship is taking place quite effortlessly. This handicraft will not die. Moreover, it will correspond to a crucial need for as long as certain problems of development remain unresolved.

But the essentially utilitarian character of Egyptian pottery is not its only attribute. Made on a primitive wheel, or sometimes using hands alone, it has style and charm. This comes from the integrity of the creation, and from the elegance of the forms. Jars and jugs simply retain the color of the earth (with the exception of those from Sinai, which are black) and often have neither exterior varnish nor decoration. Their beauty is unique and compelling, to the extent that large numbers of foreigners residing in Egypt make them an element of indoor decoration, according them prime places in their homes.

Garagos

Pottery-making is scattered throughout the country, and enjoys a privileged situation in Upper Egypt, but it has found a completely new form in Garagos. Once again, like the weavers of Harraniya, adolescents were called on to create, but this time the initiative goes back to a Jesuit priest, Father de Montgolfier. Sent by his order in 1950 to take care of the Coptic community in Garagos, he first established a school, and then looked around for a means of providing the adolescents with a lucrative profession. After several more or less fruitful ventures, he decided to make potters of them. Pottery, after all, was, and is, one of the region's strengths. But rather than just ape the artisans of the Said, Father de Montgolfier chose a more artistic form of pottery, which is how ceramics came to be made in Garagos.

Once the objective was defined, the Jesuit put the project into the hands of two men. Robert de Montgolfier, his nephew, a potter by profession, would begin the training of the young apprentices, while Hassan Fathy, the founder of the famous village of Gurna, would design the plans for workshops along the lines of the traditional architecture of Upper Egypt.

Thus, a thoroughly modern pottery center was established in Garagos in 1956, equipped with sophisticated wheels and powerful kilns, making it as well-endowed with materials as it was in manpower. Many young people responded to the call, among them those who had not shown great academic abilities at school, as well as others who expressed a specific interest in the trade. At this stage, Father Philip Ackermann succeeded Father de Montgolfier, and a turn of the wheel of fortune projected him into the role of true founder of Garagos. The reason is that towards the end of 1956, after the Suez War, most French civilians were expelled from Egypt. Those in religious orders were permitted to remain. Thus, Robert de Montgolfier had to return to France and Father Ackermann was left to pursue the task alone. All the same, he loved it! The village children surrounding him manifested real talent. They were docile, enthusiastic and very receptive. At the time when he took total charge of the workshops, the potters already knew how to use the wheel with dexterity, and to make rudimentary vases. They improved very quickly. To complete their training, he taught them some general notions of pottery, and showed them illustrated works on what was being made elsewhere in the world. They learned to recognize shapes other than those which their own hands formed spontaneously. He also revealed to them the riches of their own heredity by instilling in them the basics of Coptic art. This art form was to become their principal source of inspiration. In this way, then, occurred the resurrection of a form of handicraft which had lived its finest hours about fifteen centuries earlier.

The potters of Garagos absorbed this realization, then modified it slightly by adding their own styles, their own view of things. They learned to paint on the vases and plates with light regular brush strokes to create an undeniably beautiful, repetitive pattern. They had no desire to be trapped by the traditional Coptic style, and created a style of decoration in which their personalities expressed themselves in lovely colors and designs.

To crown this effort an annual exhibition was held in Cairo, usually in one of the big halls of the College of the Jesuit Fathers. Once again, the public was appreciative. People already loved the Coptic rugs, and now were just as enthusiastic about the pottery of Garagos.

This appreciation encouraged the potters to even greater efforts. Father Ackermann showed them where to get the essential clay, and where in the desert it was possible to find raw materials to make enamel cheaply. He also built them a kiln and a small grinder. They were completely self-sufficient. They were about to launch themselves into a new venture, the modeling of little statuettes, naïve and charming reflections of peasant life.

They gave full rein to their imaginations and ingenuity, and began to produce a series of *fellahin* characters: the *fellaha* who visits the market with her basket or who carries water in a *ballas* balanced securely on her head, the *fellah* riding a donkey or playing the *oud*. Through the years, their reputation grew and consolidated to the point where their experiments and their work earned them the accolade of having created a whole new style at Garagos.

In time, however, the Garagos center for handicrafts acquired an unfortunate but indisputable notoriety. From its high point in the fifties, the potters' products, the dishes, vases, ashtrays, candelabra and knickknacks, had a regular clientèle. At this stage, the Jesuits left the village. They had achieved their social mission, having established an activity capable of improving the condition of the peasants. From then on, the adolescents of the fifties became men and managed their businesses themselves.

Early on, the group of potters continued its work with great professionalism. Sales kept up and even grew. Then the artisans of Garagos succumbed to the temptation of producing quickly in order to sell more. Their success sowed the seeds of an artistic drama. They no longer concerned themselves with artistic values, but began to repeat over and over again the shapes and figurines which had attracted public favor. In short, their pottery became assembly-line work, eternal repetition, a practice belonging to most of the artisans of Khan al Khalili. Moreover, the future of the workshops became a 'family affair', where the only apprentices admitted were the sons and nephews.

Can we speak, in this context, of a skilled craft? If we apply the term rigorously, the answer is 'no'. But the term has nuances, especially if we take into consideration the fact that an artisan is not an artist, that the potters of Garagos, tormented by economic constraints, are not craftsmen in a luxury medium, and that the glassmakers of Venice acted no differently in their golden age, and that when all is said and done, the artisan always fights against the limitations of his material, yet still manages occasionally to produce something of real artistic imagination.

Though in some ways special to Garagos, ceramics can boast numerous skilled workers in Cairo where, in many areas, from Giza to Harraniya, from Dokki to Ain Shams, skilled potters are found recreating stylized forms of popular pieces. They are artisans who have the advantage over their colleagues elsewhere of being trained. Not only is their technique excellent, but they also possess some notions of fine art and of popular art. So they are able to pick out the traditional symbols, and then adapt them to popular taste: cockerels, horses, riders, candelabra in female form, and scarabs, are all given a new look, other colors, other uses. They make very attractive trinkets and have excellent decorative potential. The potters also make jugs and pitchers with fancy handles, vessels which can be used on a table, displayed on a shelf, or even serve as the base of a lamp. They also make tea services, coffee and liqueur sets, plates and cooking pots, all of the pieces required for a complete set of crockery. Sometimes, the artisan paints Koranic verses or proverbs on the vases and plates, and occasionally the same phrases are finely chiseled onto the pieces. Unfortunately, the use of molds is not always excluded, a practice from which the young people of Garagos can be absolved, at least.

Many modern potters are well-known for their small folkloric figures portraying peasants, dancers, musicians, and various people of rustic life. (See color illustration 15.) This is how the artist–artisans of Cairo preserve tradition in the very heart of a capital which lives at a frantic pace. This link with the past confers a very particular style on their works—just one of their many qualities.

Other potters have risen above the mundane level, to give Egyptian pottery a place in the realm of fine art. In the last fifteen years or so, some fine craftsmen have established studios at Harraniya or along the road leading there. Others have set up in Fustat, the heart of this ancient craft, and in the Fayoum, among ordinary working people. These potters are not artisans in the strictest sense of the word; they combine their heritage of an artistic culture with their own desire to produce beautiful objects. They strive to preserve tradition by enriching it with their own imaginations, and their success is evident in the undoubted beauty of the objects they produce.

WHERE TO FIND

Utilitarian pottery
- pottery centers in Fustat, Cairo
- individual potters in Mohandiseen, and in Helwan, outside Cairo
- small stores and homes all over Upper Egypt (Qena, Ballas, Garagos, Akhmim)
- small stores and the potters' homes in all the oases of the New Valley (Kharga, Dakhla, Bahariya, Farafra), and in Siwa
- *suqs* in the tourist centers of Sinai (Sharm al Sheikh, Nuweiba, al Arish
- as a general rule, it is possible to buy pottery in all the towns and villages of Egypt

Fine Art Pottery
- Ramses Wissa Wassef's center, Harraniya
- Mohi al Din Hussein, Harraniya
- Mohammed Darwish, Harraniya
- Antoinette Henein, Harraniya
- Safarkhan, 6, Brazil Street, Zamalek, Cairo
- Alfostat, 4A, Hassan Assim, Zamalek, Cairo; exhibits and sells the work of potters like Mohammed Mandour, Samir al Guindi, Mohammed Hagras, Safia Helmi
- the rustic figures (see color illustration 15) can be found in crafts stores all over Cairo, and in shopping centers in the large hotels; they are made at 261, Sudan Street, Mohandiseen, Cairo
- Michel and Evelyne Pastor, in Tunis village in the Fayoum

9

Wood

When wood handicrafts are spoken about in Egypt, it is the beautiful balconies (*mashrabiya*) of intricately carved and turned wood, which adorn hundreds of old houses, that immediately spring to mind. This image, spectacular without a doubt, has eventually replaced all others, especially because these romantic balconies have come to represent all the mystique of the Orient. The general public thinks that the essential role of the *mashrabiya* was to protect the 'harems' of princes and nobles from indiscreet intrusion. The specialists are indignant at this belief, and are always ready to describe the different functions of *mashrabiya*, which are behind the current renaissance of Arab-style houses.

The craft of woodworking has deep roots in Egypt. History reveals that for thousands of years the Egyptians have known how to work wood and make from it all sorts of very beautiful objects: armchairs with elegantly worked backs, beds with feet worked as lion and tiger heads, caskets sometimes inlaid with ivory, statuettes of kings and queens, all from the earlist pharaonic dynasties. Later, the Copts were masters in the art of engraving and carving wood as well as in inlay work, marquetry. The essential fact is that Egypt owes the fascinating beauty of certain quarters

Beautiful mashrabiya balconies, of intricately carved and turned wood, adorn hundreds of old houses, and are the origin of the modern renaissance of Arab-style houses.

of Cairo to its carpenters. They have contributed just as much as the architects to the birth of a style and a technique.

The earliest manifestations of this particular technique, that of turned wood (*khart*), goes back to the Fatimid era. These caliphs were the prime movers of a great artistic impulse in the country. They demonstrated an interest in the carpenters which inspired these artisans to prodigious efforts, of which the *mihrabs* (prayer niches) of some tenth century sanctuaries are enduring witnesses. It is in the *mihrabs* of this epoch that the first specifically Islamic technique is evident. It involves a very special kind of marquetry, made with thin strips arranged in the wood to frame small, intricately carved panels. But this work is not peculiar to Egypt. The artisans of Cordoba, Fez, and Marrakech practiced it at the same time, and with equal virtuosity. This is proof, if any were needed, of the common ancestry and the interplay of influences which have always linked the artists and artisans of the Islamic world.

In Fatimid Cairo, we find mosques endowed with marvelous pulpits (*minbars*), and *mihrabs* of unequaled beauty. These masterpieces comprise a harmonious mix of sections of carved wood (*khart*) and inlaid surfaces in a precisely geometrical assembly of squares, diamonds, trapezoids and stars which fit together like the many pieces of a jigsaw puzzle. This technique of fitting together (*khashab muashaq*) also requires extraordinary dexterity. This form of decoration originated in the mosques, but was very quickly adopted by the churches, where the Coptic artisans adapted them to Christian architecture. Tradition in these churches dictates a double segregation during the services: men should be separated from women, and the congregation from the priests. This double exigency is the basis for partitioning the church into several compartments effected by erecting wooden screens. These screens present combinations of turned and fitted wood in the true Arab style, the only difference being that the geometric patterns are combined to produce crosses.

Later, during the reign of Saladin and then that of the Mamluks, the techniques of turning, fitting and inlaying wood were formalized and spread. Both Egyptian and Syrian artisans shared in its practice. Using wood imported from Lebanon and the Indies, their skills flourished. Spectacular religious furniture appeared: pulpits with stairs, low chairs (*kursis*) for mosque teachers, lecterns for the Koran, tables and chests of precious wood in which to store Korans, and doors composed of little panels of polygonal stars.

Also during the time of the Mamluks, a kind of revolution took place. The woodworking crafts exceeded the strictly religious context. The 'turners' became bolder and had the audacity to make furniture destined for palace interiors, dwellings of the rich bourgeoisie, and, of course, the balconies which would metamorphosize the appearance of the streets. They made admirable pieces: chests and wardrobes composed of little panels fitted together and ornamented with carving and inlay; tables and pedestal tables with geometric and floral patterns made up of inlays of ivory, mother-of-pearl, and silver; chairs and divans with backs of turned wood, and so on. But the dazzling work, that which would never cease to captivate art lovers the world over, remains the *mashrabiyas*. These unique balconies, of a charm that seems to combine all the poetry and mystery of the Orient, certainly conferred on Arab architecture its own special flavor. From the thirteenth century on, they became an indispensable ingredient in the decoration of opulent quarters. Both Muslim and Christian women took to using the shelter of the wooden grills for gossiping and entertaining each other. Perhaps this is the origin of the misunderstanding that the *mashrabiya* was intended to mask the harem.

The woodturners enjoyed their golden age up until the middle of the reign of Mohammed Ali. Then, a sociocultural evolution brought it to an end. The old Pasha and his successors turned their attention to the West, wanting to fashion a modern state on the model of European nations. Khedive Ismail even went to the extent of applying this concept to whole cities. It is to him that Cairo and Alexandria owe their most beautiful neighborhoods.

But sadly, this metamorphosis had grave consequences. The infatuation with all things foreign made the Egyptian élite turn away from locally produced things, especially furniture. Great luxury, the true sign of wealth, consists in furnishing according to European tastes. The Belle Epoque favored this phenomenon and the years between the wars accelerated it. After the twenties, Cairo, Alexandria, Ismailia and Suez were inhabited by French, English, Italians and Greeks. Hence, the best architecture was the work of Westerners pushing the principles of an Arab urbanization out. Similarly, interior decoration obeyed the same dictates. In the salons, the styles of Louis XV, Louis XVI, Empire, Regency and Queen Anne triumphed. To survive, Egyptian carpenters were obliged to conform to the tastes of the day. Little by little, because of lack of demand, most of them eventually abandoned the manufacture of turned wood. The traditional techniques became the privilege of a handful of artisans who guarded their secrets.

Hassan Fathy

A quarter of a century passed without change to this regrettable situation. Then suddenly, things turned upside down, a twist of fate, as it was the Westerners themselves who vouchsafed an interest in traditional Arab furniture. The fashion was now all for orientalism, a demonstration of a passionate interest in the past, and European and American art lovers were ready to pay very substantial sums to acquire *mashrabiya,* ivory inlaid chests, and turned-wood screens. And at the same time, members of the Egyptian élite, those chiefly responsible for the decline of the craft, today avidly collect the objects which their predecessors sold or had relegated to the attic. In the context of Egypt, this new fashion was due to the bold

Nowadays, those walls of mashrabiya *which surrounded palaces can only be seen in museums.*

Mashrabiya *has a specific function with regard to climate. With its rounded spokes, it produces a gradation of light and shade, softening the contrasts. This room in Alexandria, pictured at the end of the eighteenth century, shows just those principles which Hassan Fathy has reintroduced in his modern architecture. From* Description de l'Egypte.

action undertaken by one man, the architect Hassan Fathy, to whom the Arab-style house owes its renaissance in this country.

It would be unjust not to accord a special place to Hassan Fathy, who died in 1989. Not only because the woodturners owe him the resurrection of their craft, but also because this internationally renowned architect marked the residential architecture with his stamp. In the heart of a twentieth century looking determinedly forward, he voluntarily chose to return to sources. The village of Gurna, near Luxor, is a perfect illustration of his theories. He created it following the precepts of the past, using very simple materials. With its low houses, made of mud bricks and topped by domes, Gurna has aroused worldwide interest, and enabled Fathy to express his opinions many times before an international audience. In his opinion, in a very hot climate like Egypt's, the introduction of domes and *mashrabiya* into architecture is a response to precise climatic factors. Although it may be impossible to use this argument in the context of all carpentry, it does seem fitting to summarize the advantages of the *mashrabiya* since their adoption has revalidated the profession of the woodturners.

Hassan Fathy liked to explain the diverse functions of *mashrabiya*. When he was reminded that the general public understands this balcony, or 'window', to be for the purpose of hiding the harem from passers-by, his anger was set loose. "A house is not an aquarium or a shopwindow!" he would exclaim. "Those who live in it don't have to be exposed to public curiosity." This view justifies the social function of the wooden balcony, which consists simply of protecting the intimate life of the residents of a house, be they women or men.

The religious function of façades and screen partitions made of turned wood is easy to demonstrate, as both mosques and old churches offer plenty of examples. Equally obvious are the architectural and decorative functions, since the *khans* and palaces in the times of the Mamluks owe their beauty in large part to the *mashrabiya*. Another lesser known advantage is that these balconies have a specific function with regard to climate. In Egypt, an African country, it is essential that air be able to circulate indoors during the summer. A window lets in heat and reflected heat, shutters are too radical—they can only be open or closed—and a blind can still allow savage bars of heat and light to filter through. In contrast, a *mashrabiya*, with its rounded spokes, produces a gradation of light and shade, softening the contrasts. In addition, the size of the mesh determines the volume of air. Close mesh can be put in one room, a more open mesh in another, and the rooms can be organized for summer and winter depending on the directions the windows face.

These diverse advantages encouraged Hassan Fathy to return the *mashrabiya* to the place it rightfully belongs in a house. In Cairo and Alexandria he built elegant, dome-topped villas, embellished with *mashrabiya*, wooden wall-paneling and doors of turned wood. This rejuvenated the work of the carpenters specialized in these techniques.

Following this, traditional furniture in turned and inlaid wood reappeared as a natural complement to this architecture. In short, with the touch of his magic pencil, this 'master' who has many imitators, gave new life to a languishing handicraft.

Just what was the state of this craft at a time when this unexpected revival of interest in it occurred? It was in dire straits! Even now, it would be hard to find more than ten or so true master craftsmen in all of Cairo.

Such a state should have been expected. In order not to give up his trade, in the face of all his problems, the carpenter had to do more than just love it. He had to survive, to guarantee himself a more or less stable clientèle, and a decent income. The rare carpenters who have been able to overcome this problem are, on average, around sixty years old. Apprentices in the nineteen thirties, they were trained by the masters of the nineteenth century who took quality of workmanship extremely seriously. Their sense of form, beauty and taste was as vital as their technical mastery. These common strengths should have created a very close-knit brotherhood amongst them, but what is striking is that the spirit of cooperation is no longer there. In a situation like theirs, where competition is not just healthy, but too fierce, common interest often divides instead of uniting.

Finding these true inheritors of the past today is a difficult task. Geographically it is complex because the woodturners' workshops are scattered throughout the alleys of Cairo. They are in the populous quarters around the citadel, near to Bab Zuweila, in the streets surrounding Khan al Khalili, and in the neighborhood of Midan Opera where the famous Cairo Opera, razed by fire, once stood. In general, it is in the area of Fatimid Cairo, in the places where their ancestors worked, that the 'turners' of the twentieth century respond to all the needs of their clientèle. It has to be admitted that in this aspect of Egyptian craft, perhaps more than in any other, the production is strictly controlled by public taste, by 'orders' in the truest sense of the term. Taking into account the high cost of living, the current price of wood, the long and minute labor necessary for the creation of an object of turned wood, how can the artisan afford to create for his own pleasure? It is, unfortunately, an unaffordable luxury. He must therefore obey the wishes of his clientèle, which limits his field of activity, but gives him some security.

A tour of the workshops enables us to make an assessment of the production and to draw several conclusions. Thus, it is very quickly apparent that the appearance of the workshops themselves, as well as the work taking place within them, and the overall mood, are, with few variations, the same. In the first place, the workshops are not small or badly situated as are, for example, those of the glassblowers. They are often apartments with two or three rooms, located on the ground floor of an old and decaying building. The walls of the central room are invariably decorated with samples of turned and fitted wood, offering a varied selection of motifs and techniques. These are the titles to glory of each carpenter, a resumé of his knowledge and his abilities. This exhibition facilitates the client's choice of model, pattern, and size of mesh. In the same central room, many artisans frequently work together, each undertaking a precise task. Watching these carpenters at their work, it is noticeable that they have learned to adapt their ancient technique to the ways of the modern world. Although they are continuing to manufacture furniture in the style of the past, they also respond to the needs of the present.

Out of courtesy as much as professional pride, each master craftsman is pleased to receive visitors and show them his finished pieces. In this way he can underline the beauty of the work and the prowess of his coworkers while the potential client admires the perfect blending of the past into the present. These craftsmen regularly make, and often with as much skill as their ancestors, a whole gamut of wooden pieces: the *mashrabiyas* and turned-wood partitions; chests for jewelry or clothing with ivory or mother-of-pearl inlays (done by specialized craftsmen); armchairs and divans with backs and arms of turned wood; trunks, sideboards and console tables with marvelous geometric or floral inlays; all sorts and sizes and shapes of inlaid tables, where silver threads sometimes delicately frame the ivory and mother-of-pearl motifs; doors and flaps of cupboards and wardrobes of fitted wood; shelving; and mirror frames. As well as producing all these large pieces of furniture, and just like the artisans of earlier centuries, the turners also make the chests which serve as bars, buffets, consoles, beds with headboards of turned and fitted wood, desks, ladies' dressing-tables, screens, small items of furniture for a myriad uses, minuscule lecterns, more decorative than useful, small tables inlaid with mother-of-pearl. which are used as checker, chess, or backgammon boards, small, easily portable screens which tourists dote on, frames for photographs, coat hangers, and so on.

An inevitable consequence of progress, professional satisfaction is today denied the woodturners. Their services are no longer called for as in Mamluk times, to decorate a great mosque or a beautiful church. Yet both of these are continually being constructed throughout Egypt. But the buildings being erected are in a modern style. There are no wooden façades, no gracefully constructed *mihrabs*, or finely inlaid iconostases . . . . Occasionally the artisans are engaged to restore a pulpit, or a prayer niche, but they no longer have the joy of working together on a great endeavor.

As for production, a visit to the great centers across the country reveals certain constants. In Cairo and Alexandria, the two cities where the majority of the artisans are grouped, and which monopolize the largest clientèle, or in Asyut, Rashid and Damietta, where the tradition of woodcrafts survives, the conclusion one comes to is that the situation is perceptibly the same everywhere. The artisans practice the same technique, repeat the same patterns, and have the same repertoire. The differences are of a strictly qualitative order. Another similarity is the atmosphere which reigns in the shops, and the norms which guide the diverse activities. It is simple to demonstrate them.

A stop in the central room of a workshop, where all the artisans are working side by side, is representative of all workshops everywhere, and enables us to understand the guiding principles of this handicraft. The first is clearly one of division of labor. Not surprisingly, there are several different steps in the preparation of the many shaped pieces of wood which are to be fitted together. The bare wooden boards need to be sawn to the desired dimensions, then planed, then drilled with the necessary connecting holes. The artisans are of differing abilities, and in this profession the apprenticeship is long. One can be seen cutting polygon shapes all day long, another is cutting up boards into little rectangular pieces, while a third takes these pieces and begins to turn them, indicating more advanced skills in so doing. Then the pieces must be drilled and sanded. Each artisan is confined to his own task and only moves on when he is considered deserving of it.

The second principle concerns the utilization of machines for turning. Formerly, turners at work provided a captivating sight. The fine strips of beechwood (used since the tenth century) were prepared by hand, one after the other, the woodturners demonstrating stupefying virtuosity. Today, the job of the craftsman has been simplified by the presence of machines, and he often does no more than guide the action of the mechanical lathe producing his turned wood a hundred times faster. But he denies that he is now no more than a machine operator, claiming that he is just as skillful as his ancestors. In fact, the intervention of the machine concerns only the shaping of the larger pieces. Putting them together is done by hand. Moreover, in making the small delicate pieces, which would inevitably snap on an electric lathe, traditional methods are still used. This is where the craftsman's true talent is displayed. To see him sitting on the ground, working with a hand lathe called a *makhrata baladi*, gives the impression of reliving an episode from medieval history. The crude and heavy lathe is made of a frame with two short legs, an axle, a shaft with two clamps, and a bow. It is no different from those of ages past. An experienced artisan (*usta*) can manipulate it with prodigious speed, and the rounded and shaped strips of wood pile up at his side. Sometimes, too, though not all of them do this, a craftsman uses his big toe to speed up the work. It is an ancient technique, a sort of pledge to a precious continuity. In ancient tales told by foreign travelers, similar carpenters are described with admiration` as using their feet to steady and direct their work.

Once these diverse preparatory operations have been completed, the assembly stage is finally reached. This is done entirely manually and requires great dexterity. Usually, it is the master craftsman who takes on this task because it is both his privilege to do so, and his 'secret' knowledge which achieves it. The word 'secret', however, is not strictly applicable to the arts of woodworking. To be more exact, it is a matter of

Sometimes, a craftsman uses his big toe to speed up the work. It is an ancient technique, a sort of pledge to a precious continuity. This picture shows an eighteenth-century artisan employing the technique. From Description de l'Egypte.

This boy has already mastered the skill of using his toe to direct his work.

top *Small delicate pieces, which would inevitably snap on an electric lathe, are made by hand.*

bottom left *With an expertise born of long practice, the craftsman cuts up the petals of mother-of-pearl, then sticks them onto the prepared surface.*

bottom right *A small turned-wood table, richly decorated with inlay work.*

particular, individual touches, individual application of skill, since turned woodwork, sculpted or assembled, has been perfected over the centuries following the same techniques, and using the same patterns throughout all of Egypt. Be that as it may, each business is a family concern, and the master craftsman shares his knowledge with, and imparts his 'secrets' to, only to a narrow circle of sons and nephews.

This restrictive attitude of the *usta* limits the number of future 'specialist carpenters', while also reducing the number of 'competitors'. In each workshop, only one or two privileged trainees, most often the sons of the owner, will be fully initiated in all of the techniques. Their training consists of frequent visits to the mosques and churches where they study the models created by the great masters. "The masterpieces of the past are our best books. That is Arab art." This statement by an old carpenter sums up a way of life, and it determines the route which each master craftsman expects his sons to follow. It is how the twentieth century perpetuates tradition.

Inlay Work

In the alleys of Khan al Khalili and in the Muski area, the craftsmen who specialize in the techniques of inlay are to be found. They usually pursue their profession in a minuscule shop, or in the back-room of a large store. They like to work under the interested gaze of spectators, and it is fascinating to see each artisan at work at a table laden with a heterogeneous collection of materials. This worktable, which is often also a sales counter, ordinarily includes amongst the sundry other bits and pieces, a primus stove, a pot of boiling glue, scissors of different sizes, containers holding thin strips of ivory or pieces of mother-of-pearl (sometimes plastic, too) as well as the object to be decorated. With an expertise born of long practice, the man cuts up the petals of mother-of-pearl, then sticks them to the lid of, say, a cigarette box. It will take him several hours to ornament the whole top surface and the sides with geometric or floral patterns. The next operation, which consists of filing the inlays, and then polishing them with glasspaper, will not take place until the following day when all the different faces of this 'artistic puzzle' have completely dried. The finished work presents a precise and luminous image, giving the impression of having been engraved in the mother-of-pearl or ivory. The technique of inlaying, simple in appearance, requires talent, dexterity and infinite patience—precisely the qualities of the Egyptian craftsman.

Unlike the woodturners whose number is limited, the craftsmen specializing in inlay work are plentiful. Furthermore, they are not threatened by the specter of unemployment, because their scope of activity is quite broad. They do not limit themselves just to completing the work of the carpenters by enriching the chests, tables, and consoles with inlay;

they also have their own activities. They decorate cigarette and cigar, jewelry and candy boxes, wall plates, checker and backgammon boards, handles of paper knives and daggers, and small lecterns for the Koran or other precious books. The objects which they make are very beautiful, easily carried and relatively inexpensive. This explains their current popularity and rapid turnover, and gives them a privileged position within the world of woodcrafts.

Also under the umbrella-term of woodcrafts, a special place should be reserved for oriental musical instruments, most of which are made in Cairo along Mohammed Ali Street. The workshops are numerous in this busy street, and all day long the artisans make the *oud* (lute), *kamanga* (violin), *nay* (Arab flute), *riq* (tambourine), *kanun* (a kind of horizontal harp), and the popular *rababa* (a violin with a tin or coconut-wood sound box). In the countryside, some of these instruments, especially the tambourines, and innumerable varieties of reed flutes, are most often made and used by the peasants themselves. It would be superfluous to point out that the Egyptian people, as in all countries of the Arab World, enjoy oriental music with fervor—a penchant which guarantees this category of artisans a large and stable clientèle.

Finally, attention should be drawn to the appearance, during the seventies, of small folkloric dolls, inspired, it is said, by the Russian models. Though the Egyptian dolls do not fit inside each other, as the famous Russian *matrioshka* do, they do offer an infinite variety of forms and colors. Collectors have a difficult choice among the masses of gaudily colored lilliputians, displayed on market day in the villages. The spread laid out by a seller invariably contains an *umda* (mayor) with a well-filled belly, a *ghafir* (night-watchman), myriad peasants with their tools, the ubiquitous peasant woman with a *ballas* (jar) on her head, a fruit or vegetable seller with his cart, a *tirmis* (lupin seeds) seller with his jugs, a groom wearing the *sirwal* (baggy pants), and a Bedouin woman in black with only her eyes showing . . . . The inhabitants of the soil of Egypt are thus represented, sometimes without care for æsthetics, and sometimes with great taste. Made by machine but painted by hand, these dolls are much appreciated by tourists.

In conclusion, the woodworking crafts, which have seen great times in Egypt, are now enjoying a renewal of interest. But the parameters of the end of the twentieth century are very different from the era of the Mamluks. Whereas the division of work is a constant, the introduction of the machine is a new element. On the other hand, the pitiful—compared with the past—number of woodturners threatens the future. The master craftsmen, fearful of being forgotten, are not willing to divulge their science. Even in this unhappy situation, the absence of serious competition reduces the margin of unemployment. The situation has evidently been

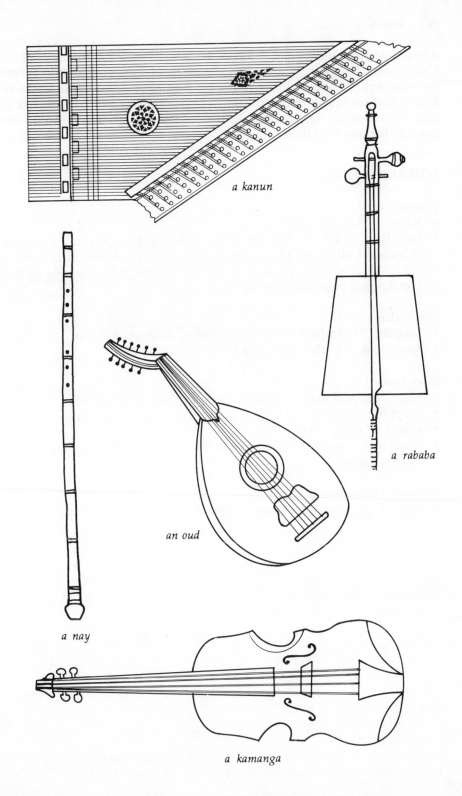

a kanun

a rababa

a nay

an oud

a kamanga

misread and misunderstood in Egypt, because in the Arab countries of the Gulf, where the palaces are often the work of Egyptian architects, the woodturners of Cairo and Alexandria are frequently called upon. It is to be hoped that some day the *ustas* will feel secure enough to take the risk of training numerous new colleagues. It would be enough if they would just gamble that much on their future.

WHERE TO FIND

Turned Wood
- Khan al Khalili, Cairo
- near the Citadel, the Mosque of Ibn Tulun, and the Pyramids of Giza, Cairo (In all these places, it is necessary to ask for directions to individual workshops, and in all workshops, it is possible to buy readymade pieces or place orders.)

Mashrabiya
- Senouhi, 54, Abdel Khaleq Sarwat Street, downtown Cairo
- Mamelouk, 4A, Hassan Assim Street, Zamalek, Cairo

Inlay Work
- Khan al Khalili and the Muski, Cairo (for sale or to order)
- shopping centers in the large hotels in Cairo, Luxor, Aswan
- *suqs* of all main towns
- small stores at all the tourist sites (Pyramids of Giza, Saqqara, and in Upper Egypt)

Musical Instruments
- several specialist workshops in Mohammed Ali Street, Cairo

10

Metals

The light which illuminates certain drawing rooms of Cairo in the evenings falls these days from chandeliers similar to those of years gone by. This phenomenon, which has the effect of bringing the past into the present, is the fortuitous result of an initiative taken by a group of young decorators (in particular Randa Fahmi, see color illustration 17). It was they who encouraged the craftsmen in metals to make again the geometrical chandeliers, like huge lanterns, made of different metals and colored glass, which contributed so greatly to the elegance of nineteenth-century Egypt. With lighting like this as part of Arab-style rooms furnished with *mashrabiya*, divans, and low tables inlaid with mother-of-pearl, on which graceful silver or copper ewers are set, the impression is perfect. The illusion of having strayed into the Egypt of the khedives is complete.

Of all the crafts of Egypt, it is probably in metalworking that the link between the current craftsmen and their ancestors is the strongest. Ancient Egypt overflowed with gold, and the goldsmiths of the pharaonic era excelled in the art of making jewelry of unequaled beauty. Their descendants, as we have already noted (see chapter 2), rigorously follow the trail blazed by the masters. In addition to this, copper has been used in

Egypt since the neolithic period (i.e. about 4,000 years before Christ), and coppersmiths can be counted in the thousands today. They no longer confine themselves, as in the past, to the production of arms or agricultural implements, but now offer a very rich variety of products. Finally, the objects in silver fill both the shopwindows of Khan al Khalili and those of the elegant main streets of Cairo, Alexandria, and the big towns.

To give depth to this comparison, it will suffice to take a quick look at the past. The artisans of the Coptic era already knew how to make all sorts of jewelry and numerous objects out of copper. Differing from preceding ages, which saw the appearance of vessels of stone, slate, and sometimes rock crystal, these craftsmen made silver or copper table settings and copper kitchen utensils. But their renown was based mainly on the fabrication of objects for religious ceremonies and church furnishings. They made many chalices, crosses and candelabra out of silver. It was also the epoch which saw the propagation of secular objects, silver ewers with their basins, curiously shaped inkwells, often rectangular with a box for the *qalams* (quills), cups, vases, and platters.

Following this, every century, or every important reign, added its own touches. The particular contribution of the Fatimid epoch was a decorative form entailing the sculpting of numerous small animals in bronze: lions, stags, horses, hares, peacocks, etc. Some decades later, Ayyubid Egypt favored the fabrication of objects in copper, inlaid with gold or silver, which bore a decoration of hunting or dancing scenes. This was the true birth of the handicraft of inlaying to which the name 'damascene' has been given, and which is still practiced successfully today. In Mamluk times, metalcrafts experienced further growth, and the most characteristic developments of that period can be found in the mosques. To provide appropriate lighting during the evening prayer and on the nights during Ramadan, the artisans made huge lanterns of copper or iron to hold glass cups containing oil. (See color illustration 16.)

The Ottoman domination lasted over five centuries without altering this situation. Khedival Egypt, and later Republican Egypt, prolonged this remarkable continuity. This is how the artisans who work in the tumultuous *suq* of Khan al Khalili, on the periphery of Cairo, in the distant villages of Upper Egypt, and in the oases, are able to draw their inspiration from the forms of yesteryear—such is the awe-inspiring and mysterious power of this ancient land of Egypt.

Gold and Silver

The most precious metal of Egypt, gold, no longer concerns anyone but the goldsmiths. It is a very expensive and very rare material, and its importation is rigorously controlled. A large part of the population would be astonished to learn that Egypt formerly exported gold from Sinai, and that the pharaohs' ships exchanged this merchandise for Tyrian purple or cedarwood along the Phoenician coasts. Times have certainly changed. Working in gold henceforth became a privilege reserved for goldsmiths (see chapter 2). In contrast, silver still accounts for a large part of handicraft production. In the great commercial centers of Cairo and Alexandria, and sometimes also in the oases, hundreds of craftsmen continue to fashion innumerable pieces in silver, modeled on the ancient styles.

Strollers who wander the streets of Khan al Khalili could easily imagine themselves in Aladdin's cave. The shopwindows at which they marvel are overloaded with vases and silver cups, platters, candlesticks, ewers, jewelry, cigarette boxes, tea services, figurines . . . . In this *suq*, where the lure of profit is the only rule of the game, silver is simply a negotiable commodity. Often, the discussions between sellers and buyers ignore any consideration of the beauty of the object or the care taken in making it, concentrating solely on its weight and its commercial value. The baldness of the dialogue precludes any poetry.

But if you leave the principal streets to lose yourself in the secondary thoroughfares, and especially in the areas behind the shops, direct contact can be established with the artisan. Here, value is restored to its proper place. At work facing the silver plaque which he is engraving or shaping, the artisan behaves as an artist. He works with interest mixed with passion, concentrating on every step, desirous of making each minute detail perfect. But unlike in the past, for many different reasons, he can no longer be his own master. The price of base silver rises regularly, while the sale of finished objects is often a function of local or international politico-economic events. It is therefore a handicraft which necessitates capital. This is why the current custom is to group a dozen craftsman around a patron who directs and finances the shop, taking responsibility for the risks, and organizing sales. The second difference, without a doubt more fundamental in this domain, is the modern intervention of the machine, and often a partial division of labor.

To begin with, a dozen workshops are responsible for the mechanical preparation of the cylinders and sheets of silver of standard dimensions, though sometimes made to order, and the threads of varying width and length. These are the requirements of the twentieth century. Speed of production is a major prerequisite, and the machine relieves the man of the time-consuming rudimentary steps. This is the first concession. At the next stage, the material is taken to the shops specializing in making platters, cups, vases, ewers . . . . The second concession is achieved through specialization. Although a single workshop could make the whole range of products, it sometimes limits itself to one or two forms in order to produce them more quickly. These practices do not seem to have affected the quality of the finished objects. One master craftsman asserts, "We are just as skillful as our ancestors but we are obliged to sacrifice to the pace of current life." The third concession is that an artisan is rarely seen devoting several weeks to the preparation of a single finely chiseled silver platter

Repetition of the same model does not automatically preclude skill.

as he would have in the past, because the cost of the material, added to the high cost of living, fixes the price of such a platter unaffordably high for the majority of buyers. This is but one example among many. The craftsman must, therefore, give in to modern dictates by dividing the work and speeding up production. A group of artisans will work together on a single object. But this 'assembly line' work—perhaps a bit of an overstatement—has in no way reduced professional conscientiousness or artistic competence.

It is perfectly acceptable to enter a workshop, sit down next to the craftsmen and watch them work. Their concentration does not prevent them from exchanging occasional pleasantries, or from listening to oriental music broadcast over a transistor radio. Naturally, this is not the atmosphere of the seventeenth century, but the scene does not lack charm. Within a few hours, you can witness the emergence of a platter, of a narrow-necked pitcher, an intricately shaped vase . . . . Each craftsman makes a section, then they are all soldered together. From apprentice to master craftsman, each tries his hardest to complete his task with precision. Team spirit reigns and is especially evident in the complications of an elaborate piece, such as a platter with a pattern of inlaid gold or silver thread, like the ancient 'damascene work'. Such a piece cannot be completed in a single day, and will take several sittings. First of all, one artisan hammers the sheet of silver into a superb platter, then another shapes its edges, while a third prepares the two handles. These are the preliminary tasks. A more skillful colleague, using India ink, a ruler and a compass, traces patterns of arabesques, floral motifs, verses from the Koran, or Arabic proverbs in Kufic calligraphy. The following operation is more delicate and requires a lot of experience. For hours on end, an artisan will engrave the patterns drawn in India ink using an engraving pen. The platter will then be given to the master craftsman, who will inlay the gold thread in the grooves. His dexterity demands admiration. It is a privilege to see him first raise the small notches on the sides and bottom of the dish to hold the golden thread, which he then fastens using a light hammer. Of course, the work does not have the finesse and detail of the past, nor is it completed by a single artisan, but it is often of an undeniable beauty. On the other hand, it has the advantage of having been made in two or three days, and bears a reasonable price tag. All the master craftsmen insist on this point, and affirm that, to order, they can make inlays like those of past centuries. They must be given the benefit of the doubt. On very rare occasions, one can sometimes see an isolated, impassioned artisan chiseling a platter destined for a particular client. This is perhaps the exception which proves the rule.

The outcome of this work is found in Cairo in the shopwindows of Khan al Khalili, in those of the area of Muski, in Abdel Khaleq Sarwat Street and neighboring alleys, in the shops and in the large hotels. Certain objects are reproductions of very old models, such as ewers, candlesticks, five-branched candelabra, the famous bird-embellished mirrors, weirdly shaped jugs, incense burners, engraved and chiseled plates, platters with time-honored patterns, oil lamps, certain vases, etc. In contrast, other objects are created to serve modern needs. In this category, one can cite silver dishes, tea and coffee services, butter dishes, ashtrays, mustard pots, drinking straws, paper knives, finger bowls, table mats, cigarette and candy boxes, fruit bowls . . . it would be impossible to list them all.

And as a footnote: could the little molded animals—rabbits, giraffes, dogs, horses and camels—which decorate tables and shopwindows, have been inspired by the zoology fashionable in Fatimid times? It would be logical to think so.

The center for both the trade in silver and its handicrafts, is Cairo. In Alexandria, the same work can be found, but on a reduced scale, while in the Delta, Sinai or the oases, the artisans principally make jewelry.

In conclusion, to sum up the work of this sector, it can be said that it keeps several hundred people, of different levels of talent, busy, that the machine has taken over the primary tasks from man, and that a certain

The tip of a Sufi lance used simply as an ornament.

These colored glass lanterns are made especially for Ramadan.

13. *The 'spontaneous embroidery' perfected by the girls of Akhmim depicts whole scenes of rural life, and has earned the right to be included in Egypt's artistic life.*

14. *An ancient craft, still heavily steeped in custom, pottery is made all over Egypt.*

15. *Many potters are well-known for their small folkloric figures portraying peasants, dancers, musicians, and various people of rustic life.*

16. The early lantern–
chandeliers, like this one
in the Museum of Islamic
Art, are works of art.

17. Modern lanterns, designed by Randa Fahmi and others like her, are replicas in metal
and colored glass of those popular in the past.

18. Arabic stained glass windows are commonly composed of geometric and floral motifs.

19. *The glassblower's workshop is more like a den, or perhaps a cave, pierced by a principal opening, the door, and minuscule slits pretending to be windows. A large part of the room is occupied by the stone oven.*

20. *Certain Egyptian painters make beautiful pieces of batik, like this one by Ali Dessouki. But the batik technique is not a traditional one in Egypt.*

21. In quality of production, the papyrus paper produced by the Ragab Papyrus Institute closely resembles exhibits in the Egyptian Museum. Designs are either faithful copies of ancient scrolls from museums around the world, or modern adaptations.

division of labor can be noted. But it should be added that the qualified craftsmen are very skillful, and their work is very beautiful.

Copper

When you penetrate the copper bazaar, in Cairo called Khurduqia or Suq al Nahhasin, the impression is one of having stepped, all unwary, over the threshold of an insane asylum. In this narrow alley, a deafening din reigns overall, caused by the men hammering copper in a sort of collective hysteria. Dozens of craftsmen, most often seated in front of their lean-to workshops, their legs braced against their stools, work with unfaltering vigor. The eye is mesmerized by the sight of their arms wielding hammers in a disconcertingly regular and ceaseless onslaught on the metal. Here you feel you are taking part in a demonic scene, or of living a page out of Dante. However, these men love their work.

The alley is legendary. For decades, perhaps even a century, the coppersmiths have given it daily life. Several generations of artisans have inherited the tiny workshops, formerly the vital artery of this artistic profession. Nowadays, the prodigious growth of trade, caused by the public infatuation with copper objects, has multiplied the number of workshops. The big studios, which group together at least twenty or so people, are scattered round the periphery of Khan al Khalili, the Muski and the quarter called Gamaliya. But Suq al Nahassin continues to move at its own pace, providing facilities for those artisans who prefer adventure to security, and the satisfaction of making and selling their products to a monthly wage. Perhaps it is one of the secrets of their happiness.

A visit to the workshops makes one fact immediately apparent: solo artisans cannot embark on the making of complicated objects which require team work, ovens, and many tools, so instead they make vases, cooking pots, and plantpot holders of hammered copper, and engraved plates. But their work offers the advantage of being entirely manual and of having an authentic character.

The echelon of top craftsmen is to be found a few streets farther away, in a part of Khan al Khalili which tourists rarely find. Beguiled by the pace and charm of this ancient *suq*, they do not know that over the shops, on the upper floors, there are innumerable minuscule workshops. However, if you climb the narrow, winding stairs, practically invisible to the unsuspecting, you come upon terraces each containing a honeycomb of workshops. It is here, in the shadows, that the artisans who specialize in mother-of-pearl, in fine carpentry, jewelry, and most notably, copperwork spend their days.

The coppersmiths work in twos and threes, making, for the most part, chandelier–lanterns like those of the last century, inlaid platters of gold or silver, and immense *saneyas* decorated with elegant arabesques. The

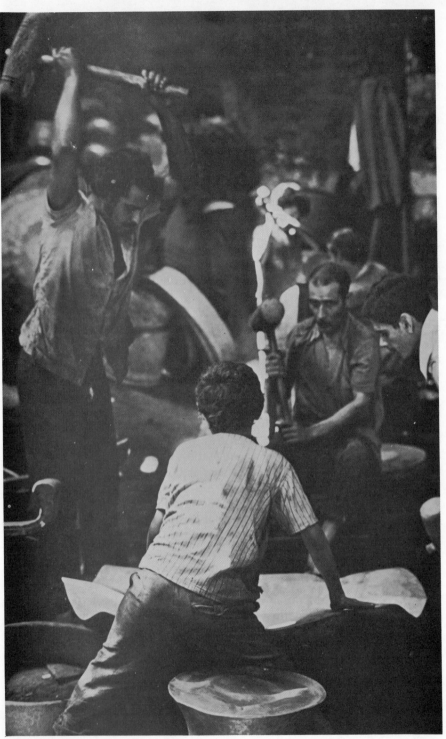

In the copper bazaar in Cairo, called Khurduqia or Suq al Nahhasin, the impression is one of having stepped, all unwary, over the threshold of an insane asylum. In this narrow alley, a deafening din reigns overall, caused by the men hammering copper in a sort of collective hysteria.

saneya is a big, round copper or silver platter, which is put on a wooden support to decorate a room or to serve—now as in the past—as a table for meals. The technique of 'damascene work' is applied with great success in embellishing these *saneyas*. In contrast to the craftsmen who work in silver but who in no way possess the means of creating such platters for their own benefit, the copper craftsmen can give themselves this satisfaction. They buy a large copper sheet with the basic contours already shaped by machine, then set themselves to tracing the arabesques, engraving them with a steady hand, making the necessary incisions, then inserting the gold or silver thread with the blows of a hammer. It is often impossible to make out the eventual patterns from the mass of lines traced over the whole expanse of the platter, because it takes a full month of work before the final design is visible. But the design is graceful and exact. And although the chandeliers and *saneyas* are to some extent the speciality of the upstairs artisans, this does not prevent them from also making other sorts of objects.

The work described so far is largely original. This is no longer exactly the case in the big shops of the popular quarters which form a belt around Khan al Khalili. It is in these larger workshops that most of the copper objects sold in Cairo are made. The rate of production is crazy, from which fact follows naturally the list of modern production techniques: total division of labor, repetition of the same shapes, and a now well-established use of machines. No master craftsmen would attempt to mask these facts, for the simple reason that there is, according to them, no harm in dividing up the work according to individual capabilities, and using all possible means to speed up production.

In both copper and silvercraft, the overall scenario is the same. Everything begins in the workshops where machines prepare the sheets, the cylinders, and the threads. Then the human hand enters the picture; the apprentices take care of the elementary tasks, some artisans saw the sheets to exact dimensions, others hammer, others go on to the operations of oxidization or soldering, and still others engrave or chisel. But it would be useless to expand on all these diverse activities, since the handicraft techniques for copper are identical to those for silver. The differences lie in the quantity and the style: the number of copper workshops is a hundred times greater, and division of labor is more generalized. The second difference is that the assortment of objects made from copper is also much wider than those in silver. To the pieces already mentioned—vases, ewers, platters, candlesticks, etc.—practical objects must be added: kitchen utensils, cooking pots for beans, called *fawwala* or *dammasa*, cooking pots for chickpeas called *hummusiya*, bowls, quart-jugs, coffee grinders, pails, scales, etc.

In the less technically skilled workshops, machines play a principal role. It cannot be denied that some artisans are content to engrave patterns obtained using transfers, or to limit their manual skills to the final stage, which is oxidizing or polishing. But this category of craftsmen does not, happily, have very many adherents, and attracts, of course, only buyers of underdeveloped taste.

It is not necessary to give much space to the objects made by alloying copper and chrome, or copper and nickel, since they are made in the same way and are not very widespread in the markets. Similarly, bronze is a material rarely used in Egypt, and iron does not tempt craftsmen very much. Pieces made in forged iron are rather limited and are usually made to order.

To return for a moment to copper, however, that metal which incontestably holds first place among the metalcrafts, the artisans can be criticized for their somewhat abusive use of machines, for their systematic division of labor, and sometimes for the lack of a creative spirit. But, in general, the finished product is attractive, the price affordable, and its character incontestably Egyptian. Contrary to other artistic professions, that of metals is prospering. The local market is not its only destination, as exportation to Arab countries, to Europe, and to the United States, opens up enormous possibilities. Faced with a growing demand, the future of these craftsmen is assured for many years to come.

WHERE TO FIND

- studios and stores in the Suq al Nahassin, Khan al Khalili (the best work is on the second floor), the Muski, and al Gamaliya, Cairo
- Abdel Khaleq Sarwat Street, downtown Cairo
- shopping centers in all the large hotels
- Kerdasa
- stores near the Pyramids of Giza
- street-vendors near the Saqqara Pyramids
- specialist crafts stores throughout Cairo
- Gallery al Ain, 13, al Hussein Street, Dokki, Cairo, for the lanterns by Randa Fahmi (see color illustration17)
- *suqs* in Aswan and Luxor, and shopping centers in the large hotels
- *suqs* in the tourist centers in Sinai (Sharm al Sheikh, Nuweiba, al Arish)
- *suq* in Alexandria, and various stores throughout the city

11

Glassblowing

Egypt had to wait until the Ptolemaic period before it had mastered the technique of glassblowing, yet during the approximately twenty centuries following that date, its artisans have crafted some marvelous works. Furthermore, their influence is still visible. Pharaonic vases continue to inspire contemporary glassblowers, while the shapes born with the spread of Islam have contributed to creating a style which is found in various countries of the Middle East. It would be difficult to determine the credit which should go to Egypt for the creation of this style; Egypt shares that privilege—for the evolution of glass techniques and the conception of numerous models—with Syria, Persia and the eastern Berber lands. Except for slight modifications, the vases, mosque lamps, long-necked bottles, goblets and perfume jars have always been similar in all Moslem countries. These resemblances have survived over time, but the quality of workmanship has unfortunately decreased markedly. This can be observed in Egypt as well as in Syria and Jordan or, in general terms, in the countries of the former Ottoman Empire. This leads us to ask whether Ottoman domination, the dark centuries of the Orient, extinguished all creativity and discouraged artists and artisans. This is the common belief. The paralysis of art and the difficulties it faced to exist at all in this region of the world, over several centuries, can be attributed to the Ottoman Empire.

Today there are no more than ten or so master glassblowers in Cairo, working in five workshops. They are all that are left to pass on a craft which reached its peak during pharaonic times, and later under the caliphs. They represent the only link between the past and present. As if to emphasize this glory, they inhabit a fascinating suburb, Gamaliya, behind the wall of Fatimid Cairo and under the protection of two majestic gates: Bab al Futuh (the Gate of Conquests) and Bab al Nasr (the Gate of Victory). Once past these ancient barriers, one dives into another age, another civilization. You have to ask the way in order not to get lost in this quarter. It is, in fact, like a village set down inside the city, made up of small dilapidated shacks of indeterminate colors, separated by narrow, winding alleys, most often without sidewalks, where you must push in order to go forward and where the shouts of children playing with a battered ball can sometimes be heard above the strident blare of car horns. It is here that the pieces of blown glass are created, so fragile that you would expect to see them only behind the protection of shopwindows. They are created amongst bustle, noise, heat, and mud, and between smoke-blackened walls.

You have to have seen the studio of a glassblower to believe the description a visitor will give you of it! This room, where the artisan works, is a studio only in name. (See color illustration 19.) It is more of a den, or perhaps a cave, pierced by a principal opening, the door, and minuscule slits pretending to be windows. A large part of the room is occupied by the stone oven, built by the craftsman himself, in a crude, rough style. Huge, untidy piles of wood for fuel, consisting of broken boxes, planks of wood and poultry crates, fill two corners of the workshop. In front of the oven, sweating great beads of perspiration, sits the craftsman on a rickety chair. He seems at home in these Dantesque surroundings, and while his apprentice feeds the fire, he goes through his paces, repeated a thousand times a day, as solemnly as if he were celebrating a religious rite. At these moments he forgets the outside world, to concentrate exclusively on the globule of glass which he inflates and models at will, like a magician gifted with mysterious powers. He blows into his iron tube, transforming the incandescent ball into a serpentine vase or a chandelier or a jar with a slender spout. What will the next object to be born of his breath be? Sometimes he pretends not to know himself, while he juggles with his tube, watching intently the materialization of one of those forms to which he holds the secret. This is, without a doubt, one of the most intriguing aspects of the procedure, where the craftsman is both generator of and spectator to the miracle of creation.

It is difficult to estimate the amount of preliminary work required for this moment of creation, which appears so spontaneous. In the early morning, it is necessary to heat the oven for a good two

By the eighteenth century, glassblowing was already a waning craft, but this illustration serves to show the similarities between techniques then and now. From Description de l'Egypte.

The glassblower sits on a rickety chair in front of the oven. He seems at home in his Dantesque surroundings, and while his colleague feeds the fire, he goes through his paces, repeated a thousand times a day.

The glassmaker concentrates exclusively on the globule of glass, which he models at will, like a magician gifted with mysterious powers.

hours. For that, any kind of wood can be used, as long as it is not green or painted, since the burning of paint changes the quality of the glass. Once this is accomplished, the craftsman places bits of glass into a cavity (called *tagin*, *bawtaqa*, or *halla*) in the bottom of the oven, where they will be transformed into a molten ball of dough-like consistency. It requires another two hours to obtain this result. Coloring the ball presents a curious problem for a country which has witnessed a thousand-year tradition of glassblowing. The master blowers of Egypt no longer know how to create more than two colors: blue and violet. The second surprising point is that the craftsmen follow no scientific formulae to obtain the desired intensity of blue. They simply add copper oxide to the transparent ball of glass, measuring quantity by eye alone. They do the same with the magnesium powder used for the production of violet tones. To get green, brown or dark blue, they simply buy and reuse shards of bottles thrown away by breweries or carbonated drinks factories. Amazing but true. These glassblowers make no effort to experiment with dyes or to prepare colors themselves, largely, no doubt, because of a dearth of available chemicals and simple lack of funds. On the other hand, they do exert their talents in turning the 'dough' on the *kajak* (an iron bar with one of the ends turned back), and in holding it over the cavity in the oven to let air into it, so producing the bubbles which give the character to the objects of blown glass.

At this point, the fun begins. The master blower sits opposite the oven at a table with a marble surface. It is on this table that the cooling of the molten glass will begin, followed by the blowing and the making of bases. With a quick look, the craftsman checks the tools placed on his left. Everything is there: the hemispheric support, the tongs, the *kajak*, the tweezers, the blowing tube, scissors and other tools.

It is virtually impossible to describe in mere words the speed and dexterity involved in the modeling stage. The skill of an Egyptian master glassblower is stupefying. It takes just seconds for him to plunge his blowing tube into the ball of molten glass, twist it expertly to collect the precise amount he needs to make the object he has in mind, and withdraw the tube from the oven. He then immediately goes on to the second operation. Once again it takes just a matter of seconds. He rolls the piece of molten glass on the marble to balance its weight and mass around the tube, which acts as an axis. Then he begins to blow into the tube while turning the glass on the marble. Next, he holds the tube vertically, so that the growing glass shape swings like a pendulum as he begins blowing once again. At the same time he uses the tongs, to shape the neck of the vase which is forming, then adds handles or perhaps a serpentine decoration.

The two forms most often created with the tourist in mind are the vases with handles or those with a serpentine design. You see them in all the workshops, just as you quickly realize that the working conditions are identical for all of the glassblowers. The workshops are all the same, the

He blows into his iron tube, transforming the incandescent ball, and watching intently the materialization of one of those forms to which he holds the secret.   Photograph: R. Neil Hewison

Glassblowers have added modern shapes to those inspired by tradition, in order to satisfy current demand. Photograph: African Profiles

blowing techniques are the same, and so are the problems facing all the craftsmen.

Each master glassblower can model about sixty forms at the very least: open or covered pharaonic vases, with one or two handles, with square bases, mosque vases, Arabian vases, serpentine vases, chandeliers, little Arabian pitchers with lids, various candlesticks, small inclining oil and vinegar bottles with handles, glasses in the shape of lotus flowers . . . all these are part of his daily output. In addition, glassblowers have added modern shapes to those inspired by tradition, in order to satisfy current demand. These include carafes, sugar bowls, teapots, coffeepots, ashtrays, finger bowls, oil bottles, tea and chocolate cups, glasses for beer, water, wine, liqueur or whisky, and champagne goblets. Without forgetting the past, they have adapted themselves to the demands of the twentieth century. They also claim to be able to make any specially ordered item, from the simplest to the most complicated.

You cannot tire of watching a glassblower manipulating his iron tube and imposing his will on molten matter. All these craftsmen can work with or without models, using the skills taught them by their fathers, skills fixed firmly in their memories, and which are the production secrets which they will divulge only to their own children. In this trade, perhaps more than in any other, these trade secrets are particularly jealously guarded. Even if, in spite of what the blowers say, the forms seem almost identical, their methods of preparing and working the molten glass differ from one workshop to the next. These differences may be imperceptible to the uninitiated, but they are the pride of each artisan. Sons are conscripted as apprentices into the shop. The physical effort required in this trade excludes women, who would be incapable of manipulating the blowing tube successfully. The young apprentices back up the glassmaker, by performing the secondary tasks: lighting and stoking the oven, chopping wood, while constantly watching him at work. Day after day, they memorize the lines of the shapes and the techniques of execution. This is, however, on condition that they truly want to follow the example of their father. Today, the law of succession is no longer adhered to without exception, and many apprentices renounce the trade halfway through their training, as it imposes an enormous amount of work and offers in return only meager compensation.

The craftsman in glass today really falls victim to two evils of unequal importance, neither of which, it seems, he is capable of overcoming. He is easy prey to the local merchants, although they are the lesser evil when compared with the all-powerful enemy, the glass industry.

For very low prices, the glassmaker turns over his weekly production— 1,000 to 1,500 items depending on their dimensions—to the merchants who have given him orders. He personally has little direct contact with his clientèle. Not many buyers go stumbling around in the Gamaliya quarter just to get a better deal on a vase or carafe. The difference in per-item cost is minimal, but with respect to total weekly production it becomes significant. The artisan is at the mercy of the traders, who abuse their advantage unscrupulously.

The second problem is far more serious. Previously the glassmaker was indispensable. He ceased to be so from the moment the glass industry set up in business. Every day, factories produce thousands of glasses, carafes, vases, bowls, cups, and various other objects at fearfully competitive prices. The glassmakers have lost the greater part of their local clientèle, and it has dealt them a mortal blow. Their only Egyptian buyers now are those with a sense of nostalgia: the lady who continues to prefer to keep her kohl in blown glass (*makhala*) or to use glass funnels to extract rose water or orange-blossom water. The number of Egyptian art lovers who put blown-glass objects in their houses is still quite small. To survive, the glassmakers have only one hope: the fact that tourists and foreigners living in Egypt all appreciate a long-necked vase or an Arabian-style lamp. Since they now address themselves essentially to this clientèle, the glassmakers have added the styles dictated by Western tastes to their repertoire.

There is one art form that could have improved the condition of the glassmakers. But it has passed them by. It is the art of painting on blown-glass objects, a technique popular in the past. They seem to want to do no more than to produce their pieces of glass, which other artists are incapable of doing. However, these other artists take up their paintbrushes and paint Islamic motifs, or Koranic verses and proverbs, or delicate arabesques on the fine plates or mosque lamps produced by the glassblowers. Previously, the painted objects were given a layer of enamel, and magnificent lamps of enameled glass were produced, and are still to be found in certain mosques, or in the Museum of Islamic Art. But the artisans of the twentieth century have forgotten, or perhaps they no longer know how to apply, the instructions which guided their ancestors in doing a second firing. The result of this is that, in general, artists today simply use indelible colors.

If enameled glass is indeed rare today, it can at least be said that modern painters no longer confine themselves to religious motifs. They do continue to paint them, because of tradition or out of love for the past, but they also decorate the objects with biblical or pharaonic images, with flowers or small animals inspired by popular art, or even with very modern designs. Several painters have applied themselves successfully to this task. Unfortunately, this artistic intervention, which increases the price of blown glass, does not affect the glassmakers. How can they gain more once they have sold their vases and plates to merchants or to the artists themselves? So the glassmakers are fighting their battle alone. To what extent will their efforts pay off? Without a radical remedy, or a miraculous interest in their work, how will they evolve, how will they survive?

This is the overwhelming problem. The survival of a craft which began several thousand years ago, but is now disappearing, depends on finding a solution. Already the master glassmakers have lost much of the science and technique of their ancestors; tomorrow they may have ceased to exist. Will their cry of desperation be heard?

WHERE TO FIND

Studios
* the Gamaliya area of Cairo: go through Bab al Futuh, along Biriqdar Street, and into al Tahhan Street. The three oldest family glassblowing businesses are all here, and the al Tahhan family, which has practiced the art for generations, has given its name to the street. It is possible to see the glassblowers at work, and to buy pieces.
* two studios near the Qaitbai Necropolis
* Geziret Mohammed fil Warak, near Imbaba

Outlets
* Khan al Khalili and the Muski, Cairo
* Kerdasa
* stores near the Pyramids of Giza and Saqqara
* works of painted glass, by artists like Mohammed Said and Ikram Ammar, can be found in all the specialist crafts stores

12

Stained Glass

In certain mosques in Egypt, the only light to fall on the faithful comes through multi-colored images of flowers, or geometric figures interlaced with verses from the Koran. (See color illustration 18.) This is also true in some churches in Egypt where depictions in stained glass of the legendary Saint George slaying the dragon can be found, along with crosses, chalices, bunches of grapes, faces of saints and angels. These stained-glass windows, called *zugag muashaq*, have a very particular style, different from their Western counterparts. The difference is that the artisan does not set the glass into a lead framework, but into molded plaster, a material which demands the skill of a sculptor from him.

In the heart of a civilization which has initiated so many art forms, the artisan in stained glass continues to practice his thousand-year-old technique. It is not impossible to watch him work, providing you make an appointment first. This is understandable. Stained glass is not turned out like pottery in front of dozens of spectators. Progress from one stage to the next is slow, requiring as much patience as attention to detail. But in his studio, which is quite different from that of a master glassblower, the artist is quite willing to show his skills to anyone seriously interested in his work. There are no secrets to be preserved. Those skills are many and varied, constituting a whole procedure which is far more complicated than the following of a simple recipe which just any apprentice could apply.

In Manial, in Wekalet al Ghuri, and in Sayeda Zeinab, the specialists in *zugag muashaq* are all to be found working in fairly well-lit, reasonably ordered rooms. The main furnishings are a marble-topped table equipped with tools of all descriptions, and sacks of plaster powder piled up in the corners of the room. It is particularly fascinating to follow their movements, because their technique—now threatened with extinction—is, in the Middle East, an almost exclusively Egyptian craft. Dressed in a loose smock, the artisan begins by preparing the plaster panel. This is the easiest step. He puts his mold, usually a rectangular wooden frame, on the marble table, which he has taken care to coat with a thin layer of oil to prevent any sticking. He then pours the plaster (*gibs*) into the mold and smooths its yielding surface with a spatula. The next day, when the plaster has set, he becomes a draftsman, carefully tracing a succession of patterns including arabesques, geometric and floral designs, and Koranic verses in Kufic script. His themes are inspired by the Islamic art which is found in the frescos of mosques, the marble panels of palaces, or simply the decoration of a copper tray. His Coptic colleague will also reproduce the

The most delicate operation: piercing the plaster.

faces of saints, or that of Christ. This choice of subject matter constitutes the only difference, because in matters of technique, all the artisans work in the same way. Once his drawing is finished, the artisan tackles the most laborious and delicate stage. He must cut the design into, or rather out of, the plaster. In order to detach a flower's petals, or the different letters of a pious phrase, he cuts gently into the design with a little saw (*zawwana*), a chisel (*izmil*), or sometimes a penknife (*matwa*). It is now that his skill comes into its own. The slightest wrong move, the lightest of clumsy knocks, risks spoiling the whole piece. He will spend days on end at this task, working with a steady hand and the skill of a goldsmith.

At the end of approximately a week, the plaster panel will have become a veritable tableau of patterns, often of exquisite intricacy, formed of empty spaces. Then the artisan–sculptor becomes artisan–glassmaker as he shapes the strips of colored glass (the most common colors are green, blue, red and yellow) with which he will decorate his work. He chooses them purposefully, cuts them to the required size and attaches them to the back of the panel. Then he pours plaster into the gaps between the glass shapes to create a protective joint. The task is completed.

The craftsmen of earlier centuries worked no differently. From available evidence, it seems that the techniques used in mosques of the Fatimid era were practiced equally by the Copts of the time. The colored windows were then called *shamsiya* (from the word *shams* which means sun) or *qamariya* (from *qamar* which means moon), because of the effect caused by the rays of the sun or moon striking each window in turn. These names are still in use. Arabic stained glass enjoyed great popularity in Egypt, Syria, and in Iraq, but it was Cairo during the reign of the Mamluks that saw the golden age of Egyptian stained glass. The captivating beauty of windows in mosques like Qalaun, Sultan Hassan or Qajmas al Ishaqi always provide their visitors with a renewed belief in æsthetic perfection. In the same way, some of the ancient Coptic churches, like those of Old Cairo, or quite recent ones like that of Maraashli Street, provide beautiful Christian images. In the past, in fact, Coptic and Muslim artisans worked together to decorate houses of God as well as those of noble princes. After an interval of centuries, this fraternal collaboration has been revived. In its expression, thousand-year-old techniques are used, motifs transmitted from father to son are recreated with a virtuosity quite equal to that of the past. But the comparison cannot be carried further. These days, sumptuous mosques and magnificent cathedrals are no longer being constructed. Congregations are now satisfied with more sober, or perhaps more scholarly styles, which demand giant arabesques executed in a mixture of cement and plaster. Simple panes reflect the architectural forms, replacing the stained glass of the past. The significance of this for the artisans in stained glass is that their work is now restricted to small restoration projects.

Apart from the religious context, the question of money intervenes. The high cost of living, which affects the prices of materials as well as the artisans' salaries, puts stained glass into the luxury category, limiting its purchase to the privileged classes. Moreover, it is necessary that those wealthy enough to take advantage of this art form also be able to appreciate it, and that the style of their villas suit the inclusion of these windows. All these prerequisites rarely come together.

Reduced to work which does not monopolize all their energy, it is natural that the Egyptian artisans should make an effort to discover new outlets for their skills. A number of them have found the solution in emigration. This carries a double benefit: it preserves their profession while also guaranteeing substantial financial returns. Not far from Egypt, rich, brand-new countries, like Saudi Arabia, Kuwait, and the Emirates, offer the glassmakers unbelievable opportunities. In the cities of these countries, wonderful buildings are being erected at an overwhelming pace, and there are also hosts of princes—to whom several Egyptian architects have gravitated—who are eager to possess mosques and palaces in traditional Arab styles. It is in these centers, scratched out of the desert, that the arts of stained glass and *mashrabiya* will, from now on, be able to recapture their past glory.

Since the end of the sixties, then, these two causes—the sparsity of orders, and the attraction of emigration—have reduced the number of qualified artisans in Egypt to a total of about ten. Resident in Cairo, the only city in the country where this craft is still practiced, these devotees (or should they just be described as stubborn?) have refused to desert the Nile Valley.

Yet their profession offers few advantages. To buy the colored glass which is indispensable to their compositions (it seems that the Egyptian blowers have never been able to make glass in absolutely translucent colors), they must be constantly watching for an opportune occasion. It is a chore which consists of pestering the *rubabikia* vendor, the popular name for a junk dealer in Egypt, in order to unearth pieces of ancient glass, taken out of an old house, church or mosque. This is because the importation of colored glass was forbidden for economic reasons, and the ban has not yet been lifted. It has forced the craftsmen to deal with the junkmen and trust to luck. It is easy to imagine the frustrations of having to interrupt the rhythm of work to look for materials, or of being constrained to use the wrong color in places, because of having to make do with what is available.

The continuing presence in Egypt of these craftsmen is the proof of their stated intention to mount a superb challenge, on which depends their livelihood, their very survival. They have in common the love of their profession, an unshakable belief in their talent and an equally unshakable will to fight. Given these spiritual advantages, there is hope that all the difficulties can be overcome, and reason to believe that the situation of these artists in the twentieth century in Egypt is precarious but not desperate. We can have confidence in their ability to find other directions for their talents. They restore mosques and churches, and are concentrating on inventing more modern panels—which puts a severe strain on tradition. In an attempt to attract interest and offer objects at moderate prices, they are adapting to modern tastes. They apply the techniques of Arabian stained glass to plaster panels decorated with wild flowers, birds with brilliant plumage, small, simple human figures, palm trees and peasant houses, etc. They then put the whole delicate piece in a wooden box illuminated by electric light bulbs. These compositions can then easily be hung on the wall with electricity substituting for daylight. Thus they can produce back-lit tableaux, often very beautiful, which add very attractive decoration to a room. By fitting together several panels they create whole screens. They also make lampshades, and, their speciality, lanterns. Round, square or hexagonal, these lanterns are always quite ravishing and give cheerful illumination to a room.

This need not be viewed as a lowering of standards, as the essential purpose is to give the craftsmen the chance to practice their craft. The danger threatens, once again, through repetition. If a particular model of lantern proves attractive to buyers, there is no way to resist the temptation of reproducing it ten times over, to say nothing of the crude imitations, the feeble copies. In Khan al Khalili, that tourist stronghold, some merchants have taken advantage of tourist interest by putting poor imitations of old stained glass in their shopwindows. The laborers, whom they pay by the day, also produce crudely made lanterns, which unfortunately find buyers, in spite of their poor-quality workmanship. It is because of this repetition and clumsy copying, that the art of Arabic stained glass is depreciating.

The government is aware of the problems which must be facing the true craftsmen, and of the benefits which their profession can offer the country, and is trying to remedy the situation. As it cannot bring back the emigrants, it is looking to train replacements. Towards the end of the sixties, two handicrafts schools were created with this in mind, one at Wekalet al Ghuri, the other at Beit al Sinnari. In the majestic setting of these old dwellings, two young master craftsmen teach the apprentices how to draw on the plaster, then pierce it precisely. But it is a hard apprenticeship and few applicants are chosen. It is possibly too radical, too formal a solution; there are those who doubt that training courses can replace the familial atmosphere of the past, in which initiation in the paternal profession was accomplished as a means to the future. The future, anyway, now appears rather dim, since in modern society the stained-glass handicraft has more or less lost its essential function: that of opening a luminous window onto the outside world.

The artisans of *zugag muashaq* may have a better chance of ensuring their survival by deciding once and for all to pursue a different direction: that of picture panels, for example. It is indeed in this context that the work of Khamis Shehata should be noted. A painter by training, he chose to specialize in the medium of Western-style stained glass. It was not until years later that he realized that his true love was for the marvelous

Arabic windows which had enchanted him as a child. He very quickly learned the technique of pierced plaster, and using his skill as a painter, he developed designs most likely to produce the best results when lit to bring out the colors.

Shehata's work differs from that of the traditional artisans in that while they follow designs from Islamic art, or else adopt very simple motifs, he drew his inspiration from the poems of Omar Khayam. His superb glass pictures are an ingenious translation of certain passages of poetry into visual images. Certainly, his work marks a significant development in Egyptian stained glass, even if, these days, he personally only provides the designs for other craftsmen to execute. Perhaps this is one avenue to explore further. If other artists become interested in the possibilities offered by the technique of stained glass and created designs suitable for pierced-plaster techniques, it would certainly raise the standard of this handicraft. Moreover, it would provide a means of reaching new markets, as these picture panels are particularly appropriate exhibition material, and could therefore quickly attract a new level of society to their creators' work.

Of course, this is not the ideal solution, but it is a practicable means of saving a unique technique, a form of handicraft unknown in the West. At least until there are more architects like Ramses Wissa Wassef or Hassan Fathy, who are passionately moved to impose traditional architecture on the contemporary world, and powerful enough to succeed. Just a dream, of course, as inaccessible as are all dreams. However, the beauty of Arabic stained glass holds a fascination and a charm at any time of the day, and at night, when light abandons the images, delicate stone lace remains.

WHERE TO FIND

- Khan al Khalili, Cairo
- two crafts schools, at Wekalet al Ghuri and Beit al Sinnari, Cairo
- master craftsmen at Manial, Khan al Khalili and Giza, Cairo
- Khamis Shehata, the master of this technique, still makes stained-glass windows, at 9B, al Gamaa Street, Giza, Cairo

13

Sculpted Stone

"Antiqua . . . Antiqua . . . " This corruption of the word 'antique' is the battle cry of the street-vendors of Luxor. It is the justification of their hunt for customers, as it has a ring of authenticity. With their merchandise laid out in front of them, they virtually mount guard before the entrances to the temples of Luxor and Karnak, and the Valley of the Kings. To seduce the tourists, they spread out a motley assortment of amulets, alabaster vases, pharaonic heads and plaques covered in hieroglyphic inscriptions. The wares claim not the slightest pretension to match the technical perfection of their originals, but the voices of the merchants are beguilingly persuasive. It is a most curious phenomenon, to see foreigners, perhaps still bewildered by all the genuine objects they have just admired, or still under the influence of the powerful majesty of Thebes, allowing themselves to be enticed into the trap. For the price of gold, they buy scarabs made only the night before, or busts of kings coated with a dust which is not the dust of ages. It is a market of deception, but that is part of the way of life in the region.

Luxor is the domain of the counterfeiter, the center of a fruitful business which derives naturally from a particular privilege. These people were

Arab decorative work in stone was once as fine as lace. Artisans of the caliber of those who sculpted windows and archways like these do not exist today.

In Luxor, artisans who whittle away at alabaster, limestone, or soapstone are legion.

born in the ancient capital of the pharaohs, and they use that fact as a god-given right to cheat their fellow men.

Obviously, these artisans are never seen at work, since they claim to be selling pieces of the past. But it is not impossible—on the condition that you speak Arabic with an Egyptian accent—to glean a few of the tricks of their trade. On the other hand, it is a wasted effort, since the work of these crafters of 'authentic souvenirs' is not very different from any craftsmen who have no serious techniques to protect. And, in Luxor, these artisans who whittle away at alabaster, limestone or soapstone are legion. They invent nothing. From experience they know which themes and shapes are popular with their foreign clientèle, and they are perfectly satisfied to repeat them ad infinitum.

The taste of the tourists is very simple; presented with a baffling array of gods and pharaohs, their preferences lean, with a sense of relief, towards those amulets which have a precise meaning. This is why hundreds of examples of scarabs, the knot of Isis and the eye of Horus are made daily. The same goes for Horus, the warlike pharaoh with a falcon's head, Bastet the cat-goddess who symbolizes joy, and Anubis, the funerary god with the head of a black dog. Sometimes the artisan uses earth to 'age' the bust of an anonymous king or queen, carved purely from imagination, to give it authenticity. But the inevitable Nefertiti is at the top of the popularity list! Her face, though in no way actually resembling the original in the Cairo Museum, is regularly refashioned. And she is sold equally regularly. It is especially in alabaster that the artisans enjoy

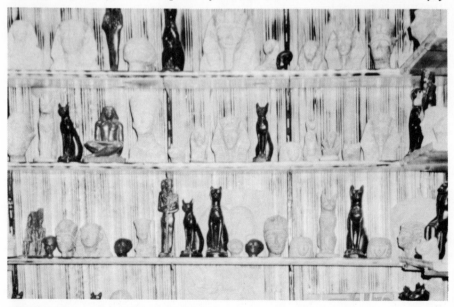

From experience, the artisans in sculpted stone know which themes and shapes are popular, and are perfectly satisfied to repeat them ad infinitum. Photograph: Denise Ammoun

immortalizing their ancient queen. Thanks to repetition, the sculpting of her long, graceful neck and elegant face no longer poses any difficulty. In fact, the hands which direct the chisel work with disconcerting precision. The same dexterity marks the production of limestone or soapstone scarabs, colored alabaster sphinxes, mini-pyramids, and a pretty homogeneous range of vases. Another recurring theme is the ibis, the sacred bird worshipped by the Egyptians because it ate insects, and so protected their crops. It is very easy to make an ibis. The artisan chooses a piece of fairly soft, oval-shaped limestone and inserts short bits of iron or bronze into it to be the beak and feet. They also make tiny jars for kohl and perfume, and tablets inscribed with hieroglyphs. The selling of these exploitations of their history secures their livelihood, which in turn, justifies their way of life. It is (to them) another miracle of the Theban gods.

Not far from the necropolis, the men and boys of the village of Gurna are expert in the art of working the very soft stone called soapstone. They transform large pieces into triangular bottles, carved and polished to resemble pharaonic styles, or into kohl and perfume jars and pots. They recreate small lidded vases, scarabs, Horuses, Bastets, decorative eggs and amulets. In fact, although Luxor is the principal sales outlet in Upper Egypt for these handicrafts of sculpted stone, the actual production is not exclusive to Luxor. The age-old natural deposits of limestone (called Egyptian alabaster) have naturally encouraged the villagers of the whole governorate to supplement their incomes by filling their 'leisure' hours with this sort of sculpting. So it is not uncommon to find, here and there in the villages around Luxor, peasants who are really quite skilled with their hands, and capable of making all sorts of objects to attract tourists.

The artisans of Cairo have not yet sunk quite so low, but on the other hand, the merchants have certainly not ignored what is for them a godsend!. Alabaster knickknacks imported from Upper Egypt and Beni Suef have made their appearance in the alleys around Khan al Khalili. And so has the machine. It is now the machine which does all the preliminary work, cutting and shaping the pieces of this almost translucent marble. The artisan merely puts the finishing touches to the pieces, polishes—all the finishing-off operations that are impossible to do mechanically. Strangely enough, however, styles have hardly changed at all with the intervention of the machine. The range of objects now includes more modern items of household use: round and square ashtrays, cups, goblets, candlesticks, cigarette boxes, plates, paper-weights, tumblers, hors d'œuvre dishes, ornaments made to look like oil-lamps, table lamps with a Nefertiti head, a sphinx, or a pyramid as a base. Certainly, the final result is often less crude here than in Luxor, but the intervention of the machine must be taken into consideration.

For the rest, it is possible to find some very beautiful alabaster pieces, though these are rare, and from the point of view of pure craftsmanship, there has been a decided lowering of standards. The craftsmen no longer

These sculptors in stone no longer have the skills of their ancestors.

have the patience, skill, or sense of perfection of their ancestors. The artisans of the past had the integrity to spend long weeks making a granite or sandstone vase. They also worked in porphyry and obsidian, materials lost without trace from the markets of today. In Luxor and Cairo, studios and isolated artisans confine themselves to working in rather soft stones: alabaster, various limestones, and soapstone. And often, especially in Cairo, the first contact with stone, the most complicated step, is done by machine. All these factors place this work within the classifaction of semiskilled.

What is more, these modern examples are technically pathetic compared with those of the past. In the dynastic periods, the Egyptians were masters in the art of making superb amphoras, beautiful alabaster vases, cups so fine that they had the transparency of paper, perfectly formed plates and large bowls, and vases of granite and sandstone polished to a glasslike finish. Granite dishes have been discovered alongside limestone bowls and plates in many necropolises. Clearly, no difficulty daunted those artisans, who made it a point of honor to dominate their material, suggesting a determination and an obstinacy which are not much in evidence today. Artisans of the caliber of those who sculpted the windows and archways in monuments like the Mausoleum of Sultan Qalawun, the Mosque of Qajmas al Ishaqi, and the Madrasa of Sultan Barquq do not exist today. It is difficult not to deplore the absence of creativity, and the often crude repetition of this barely semiskilled level of craftsmanship, which, very soon, will become widespread. Sadly, the total lack of a critical faculty among the majority of tourists gives no encouragement to the artisans to use their skills more creatively. Easy sales are, after all, the best incentive for mediocrity.

WHERE TO FIND

Craftsmen
• Craftsmen can be seen at work in Luxor, its neighboring villages, including Gurna, and in Khan al Khalili, Cairo

Outlets
• street-vendors, *suqs*, and stores around Luxor, Aswan, Alexandria, and the Pyramids of Giza and Saqqara
• shopping centers in large hotels
• Khan al Khalili and the Muski, Cairo
• stores throughout Cairo (Abdel Khaleq Sarwat Street, and in Zamalek, Garden City, Heliopolis)
• Kerdasa

14

Batik

In Egypt, batik is a craft which has been practiced only comparatively recently—which is perhaps strange, as it is an ancient technique, and Egypt is a country with a long artisanal tradition. It seems even odder if the local belief that batik was created in Egypt during the Coptic era, and not in Java, as history would have it, is taken into account. (Professor Saad Kamel, director of the Department of Weaving at the Ministry of Culture, claims that certain cloths and tapestries of the third and fourth centuries were made using batik techniques. He has published several studies on the subject.) If this claim is true, then why and how did batik skills die? Perhaps because the craftsmen of the Nile Valley, who wove marvelous cloth and decorated it with fine embroidery, were not attracted for very long by a form of handicraft which did not further enrich their output. Whatever the reason, it is only in the last twenty-five years or so that artists and craftsmen have experimented with pots of hot wax and with mixing different intensities of color in vats of dye.

Since its appearance, or its reappearance in Egypt, batik has aroused heated controversy. Its practitioners, painters for the most part, do not like being thought of as artisans! It is they who introduced the technique into the country. By imitating their European and American counterparts of the end of the last century, they began to experiment with batik's possibilities in the mid-fifties. So batik, this 'painting in wax', took root in Cairo. The precise skills which batik requires are a knowledge of the science of colors, coupled with a real talent for drawing. Since the slightest mistake can mar an entire piece, these instigators of batik reject what they see as the undervalued term 'handicraft'. In their opinion, 'applied art' is more suitable.

But this controversy notwithstanding, we can admire, unreservedly, their batiks, which tell the tales of peasant life, revive the events of the past, and paint the faces of the *fellahin* or gods and goddesses. To express themselves through batik, the painters have drawn on their own oriental traditions, both past and present, by skillfully recreating their surroundings. Whether figurative or abstract painters, all the artists have one inspiration in common: the character of Egypt. Their attachment to this country, in its religious spiritualism, its history, its folklore, and its landscapes, is reflected in each of their works.

If we allow ourselves to cast a sweeping glance over the whole scope of Egyptian batik work, it is soon clear that it takes several forms. (See color illustration 20.) There are painters who seek to achieve a fine art, and who compose a piece of batik as they would an oil painting. On the other hand, there are those who design dress materials and motifs for tablecloths. And, there are, to be sure, straightforward artisans.

The first category includes the pioneers, those painters who used this technique for artistic reasons, with no intention of ever replacing their paints and paintbrushes with hot wax and dyes. In time, this initial nucleus was augmented by certain painters of the next generation, also tempted to experiment with batik for similar reasons. The work of this group, not more than ten people all told, have put together a representative collection of work inspired by contemporary Egyptian painting. In effect, all of the great pictorial themes can be found: biblical and Islamic religious subjects, the great heros of Islam, abstract compositions, references to more scholarly subjects, as well as delightful impressions of both rural and urban environments. What these artists, many of whom were already well-known and respected as painters, succeeded in doing, in fact, was to express their artistic talents in the medium of batik. Certainly, their achievements added an Egyptian dimension to the whole art form. But whether it counts as a handicraft is open to question.

There is yet another group of artists, whose work is more aptly so described. In general, this group is composed of graduates from various faculties of applied art. During their training, they were taught the fundamental principles of batik along with painting on glass or pottery. They later adopted the technique as their choice of producing 'useful and beautiful objects' (the definition of handicrafts given by the architect Ramses Wissa Wassef). Although in many cases they composed real scenes, their essential motive was not the picture itself but the fabrication of common objects in batik. In this respect, their originality is greater than that of the earlier groups. While hard at work in their studios, they do not try for inspired visions or sophisticated designs, but rather to steadily and exactly produce designs suitable for scarves or the bodice of a dress.

Often they begin by drawing the arabesques or images on paper, but the first stage of the batik process proper is to put the design onto the cotton or silk cloth. Then they coat the appropriate sections of the design with hot wax on both sides of the fabric, using a special pointed brush. Those who draw directly in the wax are rare. The fabric is then dipped in cold water to set the wax and wet the remaining material, and then into a dye bath. To make sure that the color penetrates the fabric evenly and completely, the whole lot it stirred with a stick or with the hands. After the correct interval, the fabric is removed from the dye bath, and undergoes various setting and cleaning operations, the last being a rinsing with hot water to melt the wax completely. This process must obviously be repeated for each color. It is slow, detailed work, which requires as much patience as skill. But by using this technique, these artist–artisans make a whole range of household and clothing items: dresses, skirts, scarves, shirts, tablecloths, tapestries, bedspreads, and lengths of fabric. Even if the sort of things they produce differs little from that of other countries, its inherent character is particularly Egyptian, defined in a unique blend of patterns and colors. The most frequently adopted motifs are taken, as is usual, from the three great sources of inspiration: the pharaonic, Coptic, and Islamic styles, with the Islamic option dominating here. At other times, though, the artists introduce their own personal touches by modernizing the forms, adding imaginative extras to traditional designs, or by finding inspiration in their surroundings. But, whatever the design, it has to be said that Egyptian batik is immediately recognizable. Tablecloths with borders worked in arabesques, or dresses embellished with patterns inspired by the models of the oases, are quite unlike batik work from anywhere else. And the colors used are reminiscent of those found in ancient wall paintings and palace ceilings, and so add to their originality.

All the same, and rather surprisingly—as the batik technique is taught in three faculties in Cairo (the Faculty of Applied Art, the Faculty of Educative Art, and the American University in Cairo)—it is not widely practiced in Egypt. This may well be because it requires materials which are difficult to obtain here, such as chemical dyes. Perhaps it is also because this technique demands a special interest in working with wax, a particular sort of manual dexterity, and a certain physical endurance. Added to which, it is not an insignificant fact that batik work does not attract a wide range of clients, but only a small self-defined group of people with an interest in it. For now, then, there is not much likelihood of it becoming a popular craft.

These limitations, however, have not deterred the Wissa Wassef workshop from teaching batik to its weavers, both adults and children. The experiment seemed attractive to those in charge, as it offered another, unusual medium of expression to illiterate but imaginative artisans. This opportunity to discover new materials, explore their possibilities and limits, has enabled the adults to compose vast scenes, designs for tablecloths and curtains, in which geometric designs, flowers, trees, animals and birds are juxtaposed. But once again, the prize for creative impetus must go to the children. In addition to the sheer pleasure they derive from drawing their ideas on fabric, batik allows them the glorious fun of sloshing their designs about in dye, and of playing with brushes and hot wax. All this joy could not but result in delightful compositions, providing that some talent is present. The children work mostly on small squares which serve as cushion covers, napkins, or decorations for children's rooms. The pieces of batik they make, like their weavings, are fresh and original. They recreate the animal world with imaginative fantasy, and in vivid, shimmering colors. The vagabond imagination of the children ranges unhindered, sometimes surrounding a central subject of, say, a donkey, giraffe, or gazelle with large circles of birds or ducklings. Sometimes, all available space is devoured in burlesque disorder, while at other times, the work is characterized by beautiful attempts to put their ideas into regular patterns.

Apart from these descriptions of Egyptian batik, one wonders about the future of the technique in this country. Although it is very common in Indonesia, India, and China, it seems unlikely that it will ever achieve the same popularity in Egypt. Batik does not belong to the local tradition and has no chance of becoming a national handicraft. The *fellahin*, accustomed to practicing forms of handicraft passed down from father to son, are unlikely to be tempted by an innovation which answers no vital need. They have always woven their blankets, rugs or clothing, and cannot imagine an alternative. The *fellaha*, in particular, will never exchange her embroidered wedding dress for a batik dress, nor her bright and gaily colored flowery dresses for what is, to her, a rather dull fabric by comparison. And on a purely practical level, the procedure requires essential materials, like dyes and wax, which are unavailable to them. It is safe to conclude, therefore, that this handicraft holds no charm for the Egyptian peasant woman.

Having thus disposed of the unlikely adoption of batik work in a rural setting—which, after all, is the natural source of most crafts—it is just worth wondering if batik has a chance of gaining popularity through art and trade schools. But those in charge of these institutions naturally prefer to train their pupils in handicraft techniques which perpetuate tradition, and to use readily available, locally produced materials. So, batik is only taught in the faculties of applied art, and in certain private schools and workshops. It will remain the privilege of a relatively small group of painters and a rather specialized group of artisans. If, indeed, it has more chance of surviving than glassblowing, Arabic stained glass, and turned wood, it will still not reflect the spirit of the people. It will never be more than what might be called 'a laboratory craft'.

WHERE TO FIND

- Ramses Wissa Wassef Center at Harraniya
- Faculty of Applied Art in Giza
- studio of Ali Dessouki (where the artist works, and sometimes gives classes) in Wekalet al Ghuri, near al Azhar, Cairo
- Safarkhan, 6, Brazil Street, Zamalek, Cairo
- Senouhi, 54 Abdel Khaleq Sarwat Street, downtown Cairo
- artists like Gamal Lamie, Abd al Nasser Shiha, exhibit in galleries like Safarkhan and Senouhi.

15

Papyrus

It is on an island which bears the biblical name of Jacob's Island, that the ancient handicraft of making paper from papyrus has been revived. For ten centuries, this paper on which the pharaohs set down their commands, and scholars preserved their knowledge and revelations, had totally disappeared from Egypt. The secrets of making it had also not survived beyond the pharaonic period. More disastrous still, the papyrus plant itself had disappeared from Egypt.

It seems now that it needed nothing less than the intervention of fate to resurrect papyrus, which was once the emblem of Lower Egypt. It did not happen until Dr. Hassan Ragab, then Egyptian Ambassador to China, became interested in the fabrication of handmade paper. After seeing the work of Chinese craftsmen, who used bamboo, he began to dream of reviving the handicraft of his ancestors, using papyrus, a name which immediately conjures up the civilization of the pharaohs.

However, in spite of this legendary reputation, there no longer remained a single shoot of papyrus along the banks of the Nile! This total extinction was particularly strange because the ancient Egyptians did not only use papyrus for making paper, but transformed newly cut stalks into string and thread, sandals for priests, delicate boxes, mats, and used it in mattresses, which served either as seats or beds. The dried stalks were even used to make small boats for fishing and hunting. And we should also mention the less well-known use of the lower, tender parts of the stalk, rich in sugar and starch, which were eaten and greatly appreciated by the peasants.

In spite of its multiple uses, this plant had finally ceased to belong to the Egyptian landscape. There are several reasons for this. In the tenth century, the Arabs introduced the Chinese method of papermaking, from a paste of fiber, rags, and vegetable residue. It was a much more economical method, and it is still in use. In addition, the many objects previously made from papyrus were more easily made with hemp, straw or leather. From neglect, papyrus roots gradually rotted and died everywhere, to the extent that many guidebooks still write descriptions like, "Papyrus: aquatic plant, today completely extinct in Egypt." However, this information has been incorrect now for more than fifteen years.

In 1962, on his return to Cairo, Dr. Hassan Ragab looked for a way to attain his ambition. He had trained and practiced as an electrical engineer, became Secretary of State to the War Ministry, and was finally sent as Ambassador to China; none of these three functions presaged the role he would play as a pioneer in handicrafts. But he had a taste for research, especially into ancient cults. It seemed to him, that to revive the art of making paper from papyrus was in the interest of Egypt's prestige. He did not hesitate to throw himself into the venture, which nonetheless aroused general skepticism. There were two initial problems to deal with. First of all, the plant itself no longer existed in Egypt, but it could be found in Sudan, where it grew wild. The second obstacle was far more serious: how was he to make a sheet of papyrus paper? How was he to uncover the secret of the ancient techniques when there existed no precise text to guide him?

In short, he had to start from scratch.

Papyrus cuttings were imported from Sudan and replanted around the edges of a small pond. That was simple. But then it was necessary to proceed gently, carefully, to reestablish the growing cycle of the plant,

This scene from a tomb in Giza shows papyrus being carried and made into a boat. From Description de l'Egypte.

always dependent on weather conditions. He finally succeeded in achieving the results that can be seen today, of fields of papyrus, robust in spite of their frail appearance, which are harvested once a year from June to September. The stalks are gathered by uprooting them, following an ancient practice, as immortalized by a painting from that time.

Then the real experiment began. Of course, botanical textbooks describe the plant and give general instructions on its cultivation, but these books stop there; they give no information on the manufacture of the papyrus scrolls of ancient Egypt. Definitive instructions for papermaking could not be found anywhere. During his research, Hassan Ragab discovered that even Pliny the Elder, the author of an essay on papyrus, had never visited Egypt and had never even seen the plant! His report, written from hearsay, had also been reinterpreted and translated so many times that it no longer corresponded to any reality.

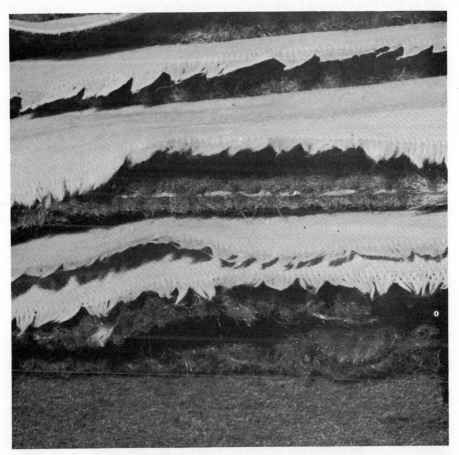

Sheets of papyrus layered between lengths of protective cotton and absorbent felt, ready for the press.

How could this age-old enigma be solved? Using the (incomplete) information that was available to him as his starting point, Dr. Ragab settled down to work. He knew that the stalk had to be stripped and the white pith cut into strips. But a whole technique had to be rediscovered. It took him six years of trial and error before he could produce sheets similar to those used by the ancient scribes. That had been his aim, and if the result that he succeeded in producing was not identical to that of the ancient Egyptians, it resembled very closely the examples of papyrus found in the Egyptian Museum. Hassan Ragab's research in this field enabled him to present a thesis entitled, *A Contribution to the Study of Papyrus and to its Transformation in Support of Writing,* to the National Polytechnic Institute in Grenoble. He reported his experiments and the results of his work to a jury composed of experts and scholars in the field, who unanimously awarded him the distinction of, "Very honorable, with the congratulations of the jury." The general opinion was that his thesis put an end to a thousand-year-old quarrel among experts.

This certainly was a spectacular success. But just how, in fact, is papyrus made? This is a question which Dr. Ragab, who soon established his Papyrus Institute on a boat on the Nile, is perfectly willing to answer. Unlike his pharaonic predecessors, he has no desire to keep his knowledge to himself.

The process is, ultimately, very simple. To begin with, the lower, thicker, part of the stalk must be cut, in lengths of about 60 centimeters. It is then stripped of its outer skin to remove the white pith, which is the part used to make the sheets of papyrus. The pith is then cut into six to twelve lengthwise strips, depending on its thickness. These are then transferred to the workroom, which contains four basins filled with water, filtered to remove all traces of chemical contamination. The strips of papyrus will be immersed in all of these basins before the process is finished. After the first soaking which lasts 48 hours in the first basin, they have lost most of their soluble matter: salt, sugar, starch, etc. Then they are spread out on a wooden table and flattened with a rolling pin, similar to that used for pastry. This rids them of all impurities. The technique of using a rolling pin is an innovation of Dr. Ragab's. The artisans of the past achieved the same effect by beating the wet strips with wooden mallets—long, laborious work. An identical maneuver follows the second soaking in the second basin. Finally, after their third immersion, the strips are soft, supple and very absorbent. On close examination at this stage, you can see that they have become translucent. Now it is time to spread the strips on a table and cut them to the required 30- and 40-centimeter-long dimensions of the ancient papyrus sheets; the soaking and rolling processes have also stretched the original 60-centimeter long stalks by ten centimeters to allow for this. After a final immersion in the fourth basin they are ready to become paper.

The artisan will make up the sheets following traditional formats. It is not a difficult job. He puts a piece of absorbent felt on the table, covers it

Papyrus grows again in Egypt.

The papyrus workshop at the Ragab Institute.

with a length of cotton cloth, then lays down the longer, 40-centimeter-long, strips horizontally, taking care to maintain a slight overlap between each one. The next layer is laid out in exactly the same way, but vertically, using the shorter, 30-centimeter-long, strips to form a sort of weft, though not interweaved with the horizontals. A second sheet of cotton is then put over the two layers of papyrus. This cotton envelope is needed to protect the papyrus during further handling. Arranged in stacks of twelve, the sheets are then put into a press. In the past, a large stone did this job. Under this pressure, the water contained in the strips is squeezed out and absorbed by the felt. This operation is repeated, changing the felt each time, until the papyrus sheets are completely dry .

The process is finished, victory is achieved, and a real renaissance has occurred. At the time of the first success, towards the end of the sixties, Hassan Ragab's wife, who is a painter, crowned this return to the past by carefully copying masterpieces of ancient Egyptian painting, as exhibited in the Egyptian Museum, onto the new sheets of papyrus. With a deft hand, she reproduced the union of Upper and Lower Egypt, represented by the interlacing of lotus and papyrus plants, the three graceful dancing girls of antiquity, the pharaoh driving his chariot with fiery majesty, grape harvests, beautiful Nefertiti, the funeral voyage of a pharaoh, the sarcophagus of King Tutankhamun, and so forth. The resemblances were good enough to please more than a few art lovers. (See color illustration 21.)

Very quickly, Dr Ragab's discovery aroused international enthusiasm. Many newspapers and magazines published articles about him and tourists flowed into his shop. Over the years, new events played a positive role in reinstating a public awareness of papyrus. The voyage of the Norwegian navigator Thor Heyerdal, whose successful crossing of the Atlantic in a papyrus boat, gave papyrus worldwide publicity. Following this, the exhibition of the treasures of Tutankhamun in Europe and the United States, returned pharaonic Egypt to public notice, as did the interest generated by the care needed to transport the mummy of Ramses II. The number of tourists visiting Egypt rose dramatically, and papyrus was part of it all. Dr. Ragab received visitors of note, such as the former American Secretary of State, Henry Kissinger, and Mrs. Jihan Sadat, the wife of the late Egyptian Head of State, on his boat-institute, anchored on the banks of the Nile, not far from the presidential palace. This public favor enabled him to buy three boats (dahabiya) in which to set up his laboratories, as well as Jacob's Island, located in Giza, which now constitutes the world's largest man-made papyrus plantation on its 25-acre site. Nowadays, too, several other Egyptian artists have joined Mrs. Ragab in copying the pharaonic paintings from the Egyptian Museum, the British Museum and the Louvre.

There is one lurking danger—that of imitation. It is natural enough. It is not really surprising to note that these days there are three or four other operations which claim to possess the secret of making papyrus paper. The sheets which their employees produce are sold in places called 'institutes', around the Pyramids, or in Luxor and Aswan. Apart from the difference in quality, there is no serious harm in this. After all, papyrus is a simple plant, available for anyone to use as he wishes. And especially as all these multiplying attempts have the same aim, which is the resurrection of an ancient skill—something only too rare in the twentieth century.

WHERE TO FIND

- Dr. Ragab Papyrus Institute, 3, al Nil Street, Giza, Cairo
- Pharaonic Village, Jacob's Island, Giza, Cairo
- shopping centers in all the large hotels
- stores and street-vendors in Khan al Khalili and the Muski, Cairo
- stores throughout Cairo (especially Abdel Khaleq Sarwat Street, Garden City, and Midan Tahrir)
- Kerdasa
- stores near the Pyramids of Giza
- street-vendors everywhere